POLITICAL THEORY
AND THE RIGHTS OF MAN

POLITICAL THEORY
AND
THE RIGHTS OF MAN

EDITED BY

D. D. RAPHAEL

EDWARD CAIRD PROFESSOR OF POLITICAL AND SOCIAL
PHILOSOPHY IN THE UNIVERSITY OF GLASGOW

MACMILLAN
LONDON · MELBOURNE · TORONTO
1967

Published by
MACMILLAN & CO LTD
Little Essex Street London W C 2
and also at Bombay Calcutta and Madras
Macmillan South Africa (Publishers) Pty Ltd Johannesburg
The Macmillan Company of Australia Pty Ltd Melbourne
The Macmillan Company of Canada Ltd Toronto

PRINTED IN GREAT BRITAIN BY ROBERT MACLEHOSE AND CO. LTD
THE UNIVERSITY PRESS, GLASGOW

Contents

Preface

This symposium of essays arose out of a section of the Sixth World Congress of the International Political Science Association held at Geneva in September 1964. The Association had decided for the first time to devote one section of its Congress to political theory, and had accepted a suggestion that the subject of discussion be 'Human Rights'. It is customary for the academic study of political theory to include both the history and the analysis of political ideas. The programme for the Geneva meeting was therefore divided into two sessions: one on natural rights in Hobbes and Locke; the other on the modern conception of human rights as set out in the Universal Declaration of 1948, and in particular on the distinction between civil and political rights and economic and social rights. Hobbes and Locke were selected for the historical session, both because Locke is the prime source in classical theory for the concept of the rights of man, and because several important new studies of these two political philosophers had been published in recent years. The subject of the second session was chosen as being topical, controversial, and suitably international for a World Congress.

Having been encouraged by the Executive Committee of the Association to make some of the papers the nucleus of a book, I thought it desirable to maintain the international character of the original symposium. At the same time a book should have a unifying thread. These considerations have guided the selection from the Geneva papers and the addition of others. Five of the essays printed here are revisions of papers submitted to the I.P.S.A. Congress. The remaining five were written later, four of them specifically for this volume. As at Geneva, we begin with studies of Hobbes and Locke, and it will be seen that differing interpretations of these classical theorists have not only their own historical interest but also a direct bearing on the debate, in the essays that follow, about modern ideas of human rights. That debate is a philosophical one and therefore relatively abstract, dealing with the general concept of rights as such in addition to the more specific concept of human rights. Nevertheless its relevance to the question of practical implementation is clear enough, and is made more so by the final essay in which an international lawyer adds his contribution to that of the theorists.

Essay V is a slightly revised, and Essay VI an abbreviated, version of papers published, under the title 'Human Rights', in *Aristotelian Society Supplementary Volume*, xxxix (1965). They are reprinted here by kind permission of the Aristotelian Society.

Glasgow, 1966   D. D. R.

ONE

C. B. MACPHERSON

Natural Rights
in Hobbes and Locke

I. INTRODUCTION

SO much has been written about Hobbes and Locke in the last few years that one may wonder whether anything more can usefully be said. But the fact is that all that has recently been written about their ideas, by different interpreters, has not yet resulted in agreement among the interpreters. This suggests that the theories of Hobbes and Locke are, if not inexhaustible, at least not yet exhausted. That they should have such a long life is not surprising. For they have entered deeply into modern individualist and liberal political theory; and as that theory finds itself in need of development to meet changed conditions, it is appropriate that its exponents should look again at its roots, to see if there is anything in them which can show what lines of development of the modern theory may be possible or necessary.

This is particularly appropriate in the context of twentieth-century concepts of the rights of man. The concept of 'Human Rights' has become increasingly important, as well in the old liberal-democratic countries as in the socialist countries and in the new States. Virtually all States now subscribe officially to some doctrine of human rights. And in every State there is, more or less explicitly, a general political theory justifying the kind of society and the political institutions which prevail there. The problem of fitting a doctrine of human rights into the general justificatory theory is different in States with different general theories.

There are many varieties of justificatory theory in the world today, but they all tend to approximate to one of three types: the individualist-liberal theory, whose roots are generally traced back to Locke; the socialist theory, whose roots are essentially in Marx; and the populist general-will theory, whose roots are in Rousseau. In each of these three types of theory there is a problem of fitting the modern notion of human rights into the general lines of the theory. The individualist-liberal theory has no difficulty accommodating the rights of life, liberty, and property, for it was built largely on the assertion of these as the natural rights of the individual; but it finds some difficulty fitting in the modern ideas of economic and social rights. The Marxian and Rousseauan theories find little difficulty with the social and economic rights, but do not find it so easy to accommodate the earlier trilogy of natural rights of life, liberty, and property, which they have tended to mistrust on the ground that these are essentially bourgeois rights.

We may hope that a reconsideration of the natural rights concepts of Hobbes and Locke will throw some light on the possible or necessary relations between those early modern doctrines of natural right and the twentieth-century doctrines of human rights.

II. NATURAL RIGHTS IN HOBBES[1]

Hobbes's conclusion in favour of an all-powerful sovereign, against whom the individual has practically no rights, is strikingly different from the conclusions of most natural rights theorists. From the Independents and Levellers of the English civil war, through the American and French revolutions, natural rights doctrines have been doctrines of at least contingent revolution and resistance to constituted authority. Hobbes's doctrine is so different that one may ask whether he should be counted as a natural rights man at all. The question may be answered at three different levels.

First, at the simple technical level, the answer must be yes. For Hobbes's assertion of individual natural rights is an essential part of the logic by which he deduces political obligation. His political obligation depends on his postulate of individual natural rights. It is the transfer of natural rights that produces political obligation.[2]

But at a second level, when one looks at the content of Hobbes's natural right, the answer appears to be in the negative. His natural right is so different from most ideas of natural right that his claim to be a natural rights man might be disallowed by a systematic classifier. A classification which required that the term 'natural rights' must always mean (as it usually does mean) rights which by the nature of things entail an obligation of other men to respect them — such a classification would exclude Hobbes's natural rights. The Right of Nature, says Hobbes,

> is the liberty each man hath, to use his own power, as he will himself, for the preservation of his own nature; that is to say, of his own life; and consequently, of doing any thing, which in his own judgement, and reason, he shall conceive to be the aptest means thereunto. . . . And because the [natural] condition of man . . . is a condition of war of every one against every one; . . . and there is nothing he can make use of, that may not be a help unto him, in preserving his life against his enemies; it followeth, that in such a condition, every man has a right to every thing; even to one another's body.[3]

Since everyone has a natural right to do anything, to take anything, 'to possess, use, and enjoy'[4] anything, to invade any other man, it is clear that nobody has an obligation to respect any other man's natural right. Hobbes makes this point, employing momentarily the more usual concept of right: 'But that right of all men to all things, is in effect no better than if no man had right to any thing. For there is little use and benefit of the right a man hath, when another as strong, or stronger than himself, hath right to the same.'[5] At this second level of analysis, then, one might say that Hobbes's natural rights are no rights at all.

But at a third level of analysis, Hobbes must be accounted a natural rights man, and must indeed be ranked as the originator of modern natural right. For he made the decisive break with the old Natural Law tradition, in which natural rights had been derived from natural law or divine law or sociability, and in which there had been a strong element of hierarchy. He made the break by deducing natural right from the innate compulsion to preserve one's life or motion, and he made this deduction of right from fact by his postulate of *equal* need of continued motion. It is because men are self-moving systems of matter in motion, each of which by the necessity of nature equally seeks to continue its own motion, and is equally fragile, that they must be allowed to have equal rights.[6] The rights are not merely rights to those things necessary to maintain their motion (or preserve their lives): there is an equal right to life itself. Indeed, it is from the right to preserve his life that a man's right to the means of that preservation is deduced: 'It is . . . a right of nature: that every man may preserve his own life and limbs, with all the power he hath. And because where a man hath a right to the end . . . it is consequent that it is . . . right for a man, to use all means and do whatsoever action is necessary for the preservation of his body.'[7] Similarly in the *Rudiments*: 'But because it is in vain for a man to have a right to the end, if the right to the necessary means be denied him; it follows, that since every man hath a right to preserve himself, he must also be allowed a right to use all the means, and do all the actions, without which he cannot preserve himself.'[8] And 'the right of protecting ourselves according to our own wills proceeded from our danger, and our danger from our equality . . .'.[9]

Thus in Hobbes the natural right of every man to every thing is deduced from the natural right of every man to preserve his own life, which in turn is deduced from the equal mechanical need each has to continue his own motion, and the equal fragility of each. What places Hobbes at the fountainhead of modern natural rights doctrine is his insistence on mundane (not heavenly or transcendent) equality of right. Even more revolutionary is his assumption that equality of right follows directly from equality of need of continued motion. Instead of inferring from men's observable needs and capacities some purpose or will of Nature or God, and then deducing rights (and obligations) from that purpose or will, as had usually been done (and usually with the result of finding unequal or hierarchical rights and obligations), Hobbes moved directly from observed needs to equal rights.

The equal natural right which he deduced in this way — the right of every man to every thing — was of course unworkable. Since each man's right was infinite, any other man's right (in the more usual sense of right) was zero; therefore every man's right was zero. Reasonable men must give up the right to every thing in order to get effective rights against each other, guaranteed by a sovereign power.

In the last analysis, the reason why Hobbes's natural rights are so different from the traditional ones is that Hobbes was working with a model of society which was essentially contentious, a model in which 'the power of one man resisteth and hindereth the effects of the power of another', so much so, that 'power simply is no more, but the excess of the power of one above that of another'.[10] It was because he started with a model of society in which everyone was always seeking to transfer some of the powers of others to himself, or at least to resist such transfer from himself, that Hobbes was compelled to define natural rights as he did. It is not usually noticed that Hobbes's infinite natural rights depended on his model of society, but this can be readily demonstrated. It is not disputed that his infinite natural right is deduced from the two postulates, (1) an equal right to life, and (2) a universal opposition of individual motions. The second postulate could have been deduced from a prior postulate of innate infinite desire, and if so deduced, no particular model of society would have been required. But Hobbes did not so deduce the universal opposition of individual motions. He did not postulate innate infinite desire in every individual, but asserted repeatedly that not every man naturally desires ever more power or delights.[11] He therefore logically needed (and he did in effect provide) a model of society which would permit and require that every man constantly should oppose every other man.[12] Breaking away from traditional hierarchical natural law and reciprocal natural rights, he put every man on his own in a market society, and provided a sovereign State strong enough to keep them all in order.

In doing this, Hobbes was, we may say, reflecting the new seventeenth-century demands for bourgeois equality. He does not rest his case on a simple assertion that men are equal, in the sense of being equally in mechanical need of continuous motion and equally liable to destruction, but on the observation that, whether or not men are naturally equal, they think themselves equal. 'If nature therefore have made men equal, that equality is to be acknowledged; or if nature have made men unequal; yet because men that think themselves equal, will not enter into conditions of peace, but upon equal terms, such equality must be admitted.'[13]

III. NATURAL RIGHTS IN LOCKE[14]

Locke's claim as a natural rights man is generally thought to be much clearer than Hobbes's. I shall argue that Locke's claim is, in important ways, less clear than Hobbes's; particularly, in that Locke, after

beginning with a beautiful set of natural rights, which are said to be
effectively sanctioned (as well as limited) by natural law, then goes on to
override one of the most important limits (the limit on infinite
appropriation), thus removing the equality of natural rights, and ends
by admitting that natural law is a wholly ineffective guarantor of
natural rights, which therefore lose the original character he had given
them.

The grounds for claiming Locke as a genuine natural rights man are
apparently clear: (1) His natural rights are presented as effective rights,
rights which others have a natural obligation to respect. (2) His natural
rights, being less wholesale than Hobbes's, are more meaningful and
more specific (e.g., the right of private appropriation and the right of
inheritance). (3) Locke uses natural rights to establish a case for limited
government, and to set up a right to revolution. In these respects,
Locke's natural rights are different from, even opposite to, Hobbes's
natural right. All these differences may be said to be based on the
logically prior difference that Locke derives his natural rights from
natural law: it is 'Reason, which is that Law,'[15] that establishes the
rights and the corresponding obligations: whereas for Hobbes the rights
are logically prior, and the natural law (such as it is) is derived from
them. Yet when Locke's natural rights are examined more closely,
they have more in common with Hobbes's than is generally allowed.
Let us look first at Locke's right to life and liberty, reserving his right
to property for later examination.

(1) *The Right to Life.* The first natural right we hear of is the right
'to make use of those things, that were necessary or useful to his being'
or 'serviceable for his subsistence' and 'means of his preservation'.[16]
This right is later called 'the right man has to subsist and enjoy the
conveniences of life'.[17] Here, as in the *Second Treatise*,[18] Locke asserts
a natural right to preservation of one's life, and hence to the means of
subsistence (and even 'conveniences'). And this right to life and the
means of life is deduced from the need or 'strong desire' every man has
'of preserving his life and being'.[19] 'The first and strongest desire . . .
being that of self-preservation, that is the foundation of a right to the
[inferior] creatures, for the particular support and use of each individual
person himself.'[20]

Is this deduction of right from the 'strong desire' of self-preservation at all different from Hobbes's deduction? There is a difference, and it is characteristic of Locke: he deduces the right not directly from the fact of desire but from the intention of the Creator, which intention is deduced from the fact of desire.[21]

A second right is deduced in the same indirect way from observed desire. The natural right of children to inherit the possessions of their parents is deduced from the 'strong desire' men have 'of propagating their kind, and continuing themselves in their posterity'.[22] If this desire is to be fulfilled, children must be allowed to have a right to a share of their parents' property. It is the 'strong desire' that 'gives' the right, but apparently only because God planted the desire in men.

(2) *The Right to Freedom*. The *Second Treatise* opens with an assertion of a natural right to freedom from the arbitrary wills of others ('arbitrary' being whatever is not required or permitted by the Law of Nature). It is a right not to be interfered with, except when one has transgressed natural law: a right of 'freedom to order their actions, and dispose of their possessions and persons as they think fit, within the bounds of the Law of Nature, without asking leave, or depending upon the will of any other man'.[23] This is first introduced simply as a freedom, but is later referred to as a right.[24] From this right follows the right[25] to execute the law of nature, which includes 'two distinct rights, the one of punishing the crime for restraint . . . the other of taking reparation'.[26] There also follows the right to destroy an aggressor who would take away my liberty.[27]

The basic right to freedom is deduced (*a*) negatively from the intentions of the Creator and (*b*) positively from the need for self-preservation. Thus (*a*), since men are fundamentally members of the same species, and since there is no evidence that some of the species were intended to be subordinate to others, they must be assumed to be equal in jurisdiction, equally free from the will of others.[28] And (*b*), 'this freedom from absolute, arbitrary power, is so necessary to, and closely joyned with a man's preservation, that he cannot part with it, but by what forfeits his preservation and life together'.[29]

We may now ask how different is Locke's natural right to freedom from Hobbes's natural right? Both are deduced from the need for self-preservation. And the equality of natural right is in both cases deduced from the species-similarity, i.e., the organic or mechanical sameness of the beings; both writers start from the assumption that men are equal in need and capacity, and deduce natural equal right from that equality.

The great difference, of course, is that whereas Hobbes finds a natural right of every man to every thing, Locke's natural right to freedom is limited by the law of nature, which teaches that 'no one ought to harm another in his life, health, liberty, or possessions'.[30] It is because 'the state of nature has a law of nature to govern it, which obliges every one'[31] that men do not need, and cannot be allowed, the right to every thing.

A further difference, less often noticed, is that Locke's natural right to defend oneself, although based (like Hobbes's) on the need for self-preservation, is not entirely inalienable (as Hobbes's is).[32] The freedom from absolute, arbitrary power, which Locke finds is so necessary to a man's preservation, *can be forfeited*, as can the right to life itself, by the commission of 'some act that deserves death'.[33] From this it appears that the source of Locke's natural right is not the need for self-preservation but is the (moral) law of nature which is superior to the right to life.

(3) *The Right to Property*. Let us look finally at Locke's natural right to individual appropriation of the fruits of the earth and the earth itself. For Locke, a property in a thing is a right to exclude others from it, to use, enjoy, consume, or exchange it. The purpose of the chapter on property of the *Second Treatise* is to show that individuals have a natural right to property, a right prior to civil society and government, and not dependent on the consent of others to it.[34]

The right to property is deduced from (*a*) the right of self-preservation,[35] and (*b*) the property in, or right to, one's own person — 'the labour of his body, and the work of his hands, we may say, are properly his'.[36] The right to property is limited, by this derivation, to as much as leaves enough for others, since all have an equal right to subsistence.

I have shown at length elsewhere[37] how Locke turned this limited natural right into an unlimited natural right, and justified the appropriation of all the land by some men, in amounts exceeding the requirements of their comfortable subsistence, leaving others with no land on which to labour for themselves. This extended right is said to be established without express compact. But it does require one kind of consent, i.e., tacit consent to the use of money,[38] which consent Locke assumes men are naturally capable of giving. The extended property right is not, we may say, as pure a natural right as the others, for the others do not require any consent. And it is less pure in another respect: it is established by means of utilitarian argument to productivity. It is the greater productivity of labour on appropriated land that justifies its appropriation beyond the amount which would leave as much and as good for others. Because of the greater productivity, those who are left without any land can get a better subsistence than they would have had if no land were appropriated.[39]

But if the extended property right is less pure than the other rights, because it requires consent, it is none the less natural. It follows from the nature of man, because Locke puts into the nature of man the capacity of making agreements[40] and the desire of having more than he needs.[41] The latter desire, Locke admits, is not present in the most primitive stage of human life: there was a time, 'in the beginning', when this desire was absent.[42] But the desire did arise and flourish in the state of nature: it came with the use of money, which inaugurated the second stage of the state of nature.[43]

It has often been pointed out that Locke's state of nature is a social state, that his natural man is social man. What is more to the point is that his natural man is a man with a socially acquired desire for more wealth than he can use, 'more land than he himself can use the product of',[44] 'to draw money to him by the sale of the product'.[45] Locke's natural man is bourgeois man: his rational man is man with a propensity to capital accumulation. He is even an infinite appropriator.[46]

Because Locke's natural men are capable of understanding the law of nature, and because they desire not only to preserve their lives, and not only to maintain their comfortable living, but also to accumulate property beyond the amount required for such living, their natural rights are both less and more than the natural rights of Hobbes's men. Less, in that Locke's men are forbidden by the law of nature to invade the lives, liberties, and properties of other men; more, in that they have a natural right, which others must respect, to unlimited accumulation of wealth.

Locke, then, seems to have reverted to a more traditional notion of

for Locke may have equal rights but not equal access

natural right, in postulating the social nature of man and hence the existence of a law of nature. It is the law of nature that both limits men's natural rights and, by imposing obligation on others to respect rights, makes the rights more effective than Hobbes's rights. But Locke has not returned to the traditional natural law: he has put into it quite a new content, the right to unlimited accumulation.

And because he has done so, he is forced to admit that men are not naturally as social as he first said they were. He is forced to admit that men are naturally so contentious and invasive that they do not follow the law of nature.[47] If the logical consequences of this admission are allowed, all the effective differences between Locke's natural rights and Hobbes's disappear, for the differences all depended on Locke's assertion that natural law limits do confine men's natural rights and do render them naturally effective. It is perhaps not too much to say that, as soon as Locke had shown how the original natural law limits on private appropriation were made ineffective by men's consent (within the state of nature) to the use of money, he logically destroyed his natural law system. It might be better to say that in thus subordinating natural law to natural consent, he revealed that the natural propensity to unlimited accumulation was inconsistent with his natural law. In spite of this, Locke maintained the reality of his natural law. He had to do so, because it was only from the natural law which gave every man the right not to be harmed by others, that he deduced the limited powers of governments and the right of revolution against arbitrary government. Only if men's rightful natural powers are limited, as Locke limits them by natural law, can it be argued, as Locke argues,[48] that the government's power is limited.

IV. HOBBES, LOCKE, AND HUMAN RIGHTS

Can either Hobbes's or Locke's concept of natural rights be of any use in formulating a twentieth-century concept of human rights? I think not, except in so far as their concepts of natural rights may show us what to avoid. Neither concept satisfies the minimum requirements of a now acceptable theory of human rights. Moreover, their postulates about the nature of man and society (from which postulates their natural rights are deduced) are such that no generally acceptable scheme of human rights could possibly be deduced from them. These statements can be readily demonstrated.

It is clear that any concept of human rights which would be acceptable in the second half of the twentieth century must meet at least two requirements. First, the rights must be in some effective sense equal. The minimum acceptable equality may be stated as equal access to the means of 'convenient' living (not an equal right to a certain standard of life, but an equal right to attain it by one's energies). Secondly, the rights must be, to use the distinction made by Professor Raphael, rights of recipience as well as rights of action. That is to say, there must be an obligation on others to respect each man's rights.

From our analysis it appears that neither Hobbes's nor Locke's natural rights meet these requirements. Hobbes's natural rights, while absolutely equal, are not rights of recipience; they meet the first requirement but not the second. Locke's natural rights are very unequal and, although stated as rights of recipience, are not really so (because Locke admits that most men do not naturally recognize others' rights). They thus do not meet the first requirement and only appear to meet the second.

The inability of either doctrine to meet our requirements is due to the same basic postulate about the nature of man and society; and it is this postulate which makes it impossible that any extension or reshaping of their concepts of natural rights could produce a now acceptable theory of human rights. Both writers imputed to the nature of society a permanent conflict of interests between individuals. Hobbes's men necessarily sought power over others. Locke's rational men sought unlimited property, which he assumed must be at the expense of others.[49] Both writers thus imputed to the necessary nature of man a predominantly contentious and competitive behaviour. These postulates about the nature of man and society were based ultimately on the assumption of scarcity in relation to the possessiveness or acquisitiveness of some or all men.[50]

Both Hobbes and Locke assumed the natural contentiousness of men because they were drawing their abstractions from a more or less unconscious model of bourgeois man and bourgeois society. Both assumed that the full implementation of the individual's rights of action (rights to seek a 'commodious' or 'convenient' living) required a

bourgeois market society. Both saw that this entailed that men are
perpetually in competition for unequal power or wealth, all seeking to
invade each other. Hobbes made the best of a bad job by urging men to
hand over all their power to a sovereign who could impose order on the
continuing struggle. Locke, with much ambiguity about the natural
contentiousness of men, insisted that they retained an equal right not to
be harmed as long as they stayed within the law of nature. He then
redefined the law of nature to make it permit unequal access to the
means of labour. By doing so, he effectively denied the equal right he
had first asserted. He thus ended by giving full scope to the contentious,
competitive nature of his bourgeois man.

Both Hobbes and Locke, then, read back into the nature of man a
contentious, competitive behaviour drawn from their model of bourgeois society. Each writer's theory of natural rights was determined by
his postulate about the nature of man.

It is easy to see why this postulate was made. It was a necessary
postulate for anyone who in the seventeenth (or eighteenth) century
was seeking a basis for a freer society (as was Locke), or who was seeking a basis for a stable society consistent with the actual pressure
of the bourgeois demand for freedom (as was Hobbes). The postulate
of fundamental conflict was unavoidable, because the only alternative
postulates could not be entertained by such men at that time. One of the
possible alternative postulates — that of a fundamental natural
harmony of individual interests — could not be entertained because it
led to theories (such as the Thomists' and Burke's) which upheld the
old order, against which the natural rights men were revolting. The
other possible alternative postulate — that individuals may, by some
kind of moral or social transformation, become so changed that there
will be a natural harmony — could also not be entertained by the
natural rights men. For they saw human nature as essentially bourgeois
already, and could not see either the need or the possibility of it being
essentially changed.[51]

Only those theorists who rejected the morality of bourgeois society,
and rejected the adequacy of the bourgeois model of man, could
entertain the postulate of potential harmony of interests. The out-
standing theorists who did this were Rousseau (who rejected the
bourgeois morality and the bourgeois model of man in favour of petit-

bourgeois ones) and Marx (who rejected both bourgeois and petit-bourgeois moralities and models in favour of a vision of a classless society).

In the context of our inquiry, the significant thing is that Rousseau and Marx, and those who have followed in the Rousseauan and Marxian traditions, were not natural rights men. They did not build on natural rights of the individual. For them, the main thing was the social transformation which would restore, or create for the first time, a freedom that would be truly human.

The Marxian and Rousseauan traditions are so strong in the world of the second half of the twentieth century that no doctrine which is inconsistent with them is capable of general acceptance. The natural rights doctrines which we have examined *are* inconsistent with them, because of their postulate of possessive individualism, which makes men's rights either ineffective (Hobbes) or grossly unequal (Locke). Yet neither the Rousseauan nor the Marxian tradition is in itself capable of satisfying all those who now feel the need of a doctrine of human rights. For no one would say that the conditions for the truly human freedom envisaged by either Marx or Rousseau have yet been fully achieved anywhere in the world. And only if they were fully and irreversibly achieved, would there be theoretically no need for a doctrine of human rights of the individual.

We have reached the following position: (1) The natural rights concepts of Hobbes and Locke (and of the subsequent liberal-individualist tradition) are not now generally acceptable, and no extension of them can be made generally acceptable, because of their possessive in-dividualist postulates. Although these natural rights were supposed to express the human essence, and (in the case of Locke and the subsequent liberal tradition) were claimed in the name of human freedom, they are not now regarded as a sufficient statement of human essence or freedom, even in the countries where they originated. (2) The rival doctrines of human freedom, embodied in the Rousseauan and Marxian traditions, both of which rejected the natural rights basis, are also presently insufficient. (3) Some doctrine of human rights is still needed, and the need is recognized by virtually all States.

V. THE NEAR FUTURE OF NATURAL RIGHTS
AND HUMAN RIGHTS

The problem we now face is created by the fact that any doctrine of human rights must be in some sense a doctrine of natural rights. Human rights can only be asserted as a species of natural right, in the sense that they must be deduced from the nature (i.e., the needs and capacities) of men as such, whether of men as they now are or of men as they are thought capable of becoming. To say this, is simply to recognize that neither legal rights nor customary rights are a sufficient basis for human rights.

The problem, then, is whether there can be found a doctrine of human rights which is a doctrine of natural rights but which does not contain the factors which have made the early doctrine of natural rights unacceptable. The problem is not insoluble in principle.

Our analysis of the earlier doctrine indicates that the factor which has made it unacceptable is its postulate of the inherent and permanent contentiousness of men. This, we saw, rested in turn on the assumption of permanent scarcity in relation to a supposed unlimited desire. These assumptions were intelligible, even unavoidable, in the circumstances of the seventeenth and eighteenth centuries. If they are still intelligible, they are no longer unavoidable.

Unlimited desire (for wealth or power), as a universal characteristic of individuals, can be postulated accurately only of individuals in a bourgeois society.[52] The social transformations of the twentieth century have resulted in two-thirds of the world rejecting the bourgeois order. The basic postulate of the old natural rights doctrine has thus been invalidated to that extent.

But if the social transformations of the twentieth century had done no more than lead two-thirds of the world to a rejection of bourgeois morality and the bourgeois model of man, they would not have opened any very hopeful prospect of solution of our problem of a universally acceptable doctrine of human rights: they would only have increased the difficulty, by increasing and institutionalizing the ideological differences.

There is, however, a contemporaneous social transformation which can offset this. The most economically advanced nations, both capitalist and socialist, are now well within sight of a society of abundance rather than an economy of scarcity. In the measure that abundance replaces scarcity, the postulate of necessary contentiousness becomes increasingly unrealistic and can progressively be discarded. In the measure that it is discarded, the prospect of a generally acceptable doctrine of human rights becomes realistic.

It requires, however, that the replacement of scarcity by abundance be seen as a real possibility in the less advanced nations also. I conclude that the present prospect for a generally acceptable and realistic doctrine of human rights depends chiefly on the generality and rapidity of the transformation from the economy of scarcity to the society of abundance.

TWO

RAYMOND POLIN

The Rights of Man in Hobbes and Locke

WHEN Rousseau, in the *Social Contract*,[1] declares that any man who renounces his liberty, renounces at the same time his essential humanity, his rights, and even his duties as a man, he is expressing in a new and decisive way the natural rights of man, but he is barely adding more than a stylistic effect to the ideas which he found in his predecessors. Hobbes, in a paradoxical way, and Locke, quite explicitly, had prepared the way for him. Indeed, in their works, already in the seventeenth century, the theory of natural rights takes a decisive turn, decisive in itself, decisive in its influence, which has stamped the development of the modern conception. It is Hobbes who, in a way, puts forward the idea of the inalienability of specific human powers, or, as he puts it, of man's liberty. It is Locke who develops this idea and who gives it the meaning that we still attribute to it today, whether or not we think it justified or adequate.

I

No doubt it appears somewhat paradoxical to place Hobbes in such a perspective. It has been agreed, once and for all, that according to him, in the state of nature, that is to say, for man as he is naturally, there is neither justice nor injustice, and that the idea of right has no more place than that of wrong.[2] In addition, there is no idea of mine and thine, that is to say, no property, no rights of ownership, and no possible ownership of rights. By this is meant, to put it in modern terms, that for Hobbes there are no objective or intrinsic values. The *De Homine* of 1658 is no less categorical than the *Elements of Law* of 1640.[3] It remains for Hobbes to declare — which he does not fail to do — that the ideas of justice and injustice, of right and wrong, are the result of laws established and imposed by a common power; they arise from a covenant maintained and made permanent by constraint or the fear of a common force.

But in restricting ourselves to this line of thought, we ignore the fact, which is no less well established, that Hobbes continually used the word 'right' to describe the situation of each man, who, in the state of nature, is involved in the war of every man against every man. In such conditions each man, *qua* man, has a right to everything, possesses a 'natural right' to all things;[4] this natural right is an original right;[5] it is a 'universal right',[6] a right of every man as such to everything, even to the bodies of others. It will be noted that Hobbes does not try to present this right, as Spinoza so harshly does, at the beginning of Chapter 16 of the *Tractatus Theologico-Politicus*,[7] in cynical terms, by showing that this natural right belongs, not only to man, but also to all animal species. On the contrary, for Hobbes, this universal, original, natural right is quite characteristic of that state of liberty which is natural to man. This right is 'the liberty of particular men'.[8] That is why, before discussing the Contract, Hobbes considers the conditions for the transfer of rights which the Contract will produce. These rights then must exist before it.[9] And the Contract itself explains better than any other text the right which is peculiar to man: 'my right of governing myself',[10] my right to preserve my own life and to use all the means in my power to live, in peace and security, a more contented life.[11] Reduced to its minimum expression, the right of nature is 'by all means we can, to defend ourselves'.[12]

In spite of this apparent conflict, Hobbes cannot be accused of inconsistency: this recognition of a right natural to man can easily be reconciled with the declared absence of all injustice, wrong, or injury in the state of nature. Negatively, first of all, because to recognize that man has a universal right over everything, is also to recognize that everything is permitted to him, and that consequently everything is just: 'this also is consequent, that nothing can be unjust'.[13] To say that there is no injustice in the state of nature, is to admit that everything in it is just, with a natural justice.[14] This 'natural justice', even if it is primitive, rudimentary, and abstract, is none the less the first stage of justice, just as with Hegel passion is a primitive and rudimentary form of liberty.

Moreover, in a positive way, natural justice is more than the simple absence of injustice, more than a simple 'everything is permitted', with no regard for the practical consequences of this liberty, of this human right possessed by all over all things and all men. Natural right, *jus naturale*, is peculiar to man, because it is, in fact, the right to preserve his own nature, that is to say, his life, not by arbitrary means (which would be ineffective) but according to his own judgement and reason, judging rationally of the most appropriate means to achieve his end.[15]

From this there results, in Hobbes, a relationship of natural law to natural right which is novel and surprising: the right of nature comes first; it defines a purpose, an aim: to keep oneself alive, in one's freedom.[16] The law of nature, which follows, is made up of rationally calculated precepts, which have to be put into practice to achieve this necessary aim. And reason itself, which is peculiar to man, is not the revelation of the nature of things, an infallible and natural light, but a simple rational calculation, a consistent logical operation, a reasoned argument, essentially a teleological calculation. The laws of nature are only theorems, technical theorems, veritable recipes for allowing man to preserve his life in safety.[17]

This entitlement to life, this freedom to secure and defend his life by all means which are judged to be reasonable, this fact is for every man his right and at the same time his nature; it is his natural right. The concept of a right has never been closer to actual facts: the right of nature is simply this fact of nature, this 'vital motion' which is maintained in man by rationally calculated means. It is 'the acknowledgement' of a fact. Natural right is thus a right peculiar to man and peculiarly human, because it consists in the capacity to act according to reason and to govern oneself according to one's own rationally established judgement, and this is something which is in the province of man.

That is why this fact of nature, operating as it does by means of a rational calculation, and presented as a right, cannot, without absurdity, be refuted by a rational calculation. So Hobbes is led to affirm very explicitly what was later to be called the inalienability of the human right to preserve and defend one's own life. Hobbes recalls that, at the time of the Contract, each of the participants has abandoned certain of his natural rights (or rather the universal character of this right and the freedom to act as he pleases); but 'it is necessary' for him to retain everything which allows him to live and to live well: the right to govern his own body, to breathe, to drink, to eat, to come, and to go.[18] He necessarily renounces the right to defend others, but not the right to defend himself and to safeguard his body, which is precisely the object of the Contract.[19] That is a necessity of logical consistency which is superimposed on a natural necessity. To make a contract, to renounce a right, is, in fact, a voluntary act, and the object of a voluntary act can only be some good for oneself.[20] It follows that every contract, according to which a man abandons his right to protect himself against death, wounds, or imprisonment, is void.[21] Furthermore, a man cannot covenant to accuse himself, or even not to resist every attack, though it be legal, aimed at his life, his body, his freedom.[22]

To be sure, Hobbes's line of argument defines on a biological rather than a specifically human plane the powers which a man cannot either logically or physically give up. Moral consequences are not explicitly involved. Nevertheless the defence and protection of one's life cannot but widen their scope by degrees, and must entail the right of forming one's own judgement about the threats which hang over one's life, the right of coming and going, and even that freedom which, although it is as yet only a physical power that can be exercised without hindrance, introduces into the argument a word destined later to become decisive. In fact Hobbes does not hesitate to talk of the right of resistance.

Contemporaries of his who argued in favour of absolute power, such as Sir Robert Filmer, or Bishop Bramhall, were not mistaken in emphasizing the revolutionary consequence of this 'right of resisting', which is for them a principle destructive of all government, and the justification for all kinds of rebellion.[23]

Filmer even goes further and strives to refute the doctrine of this 'right of nature', a principle dangerous to sovereign authority and to the good order of the State.[24]

Filmer and Bramhall did not lack perspicacity here, even though their argument perhaps goes against Hobbes himself. For the fact is that the Hobbesian theory of natural right, both in the affirmation of this right and in the affirmation that it contains something which a man cannot either physically or logically renounce, opens up new paths. He insists on the rational aspect of the doctrine. He pushes to the extreme limit its individualistic character, in making the being who has the right naturally and radically asocial. The doctrine of absolute sovereignty, by its doctrine of reason, by its doctrine of the individual, paradoxically heralds Locke and even the doctrine of the rights of man.

II

The relations between the political theory of Locke and that of Hobbes are strange. At first sight, they seem totally opposed to each other. On closer examination, however, one can observe that there is a kind of continuity crossing from one to the other, over their opposed positions, as if Locke, in combating Hobbes, had none the less inherited something from him. However much Locke may take the opposite point of view from Hobbes, in preserving the framework of his doctrine he keeps its essential outlines. This is what is known as the doctrine of natural rights.

The starting point again deals with the relation between the natural rights of man and the law of his nature; but in Locke, it is the law of nature which comes first and not the natural right.

In fact the law of nature expresses the situation and significance of man in relation to the universal order of things. Hobbes started off from a factual datum, that there is a particular form of natural existence, man, every man. On the other hand, Locke starts from an order of the universe, such as an all-powerful and wise God created with the intention of enabling man to exist therein and of putting him to the test. This order is full of meaning for those who can understand it. In other words, this order is reasonable, and man is, by nature, endowed with enough reason to know the law of his nature and with enough freedom to become a man in conformity with his law — or to divest himself of his humanity. The law of nature is not then, as in Hobbes, based on existing functions of a given being and in order rationally to assure his preservation. It is imposed on a being essentially 'capable of laws',[25] that is to say, capable of reason and freedom,[26] and consequently capable of making himself (or of not making himself), but who is not immediately, either free or reasonable. For him, as for the adults who surround him at his birth, and who will initiate his upbringing and education, the law of nature is given in the form of an obligation, an obligation to become effectively a moral being, that is to say, a free and reasonable man.[27] The law of nature, in the shape of reason, which is that law, obliges more particularly every man to preserve his life and limb, his liberty and his possessions, and to be active in rendering the same service to others. It wills the peace and preservation of all mankind.[28] For every man, his original liberty has meaning only by reference to this law, just as his liberty, when it is fully developed, will find a meaning through the law which it will have imposed upon itself in order to obey the law of nature.[29]

It is in the necessary connexion between man's liberty and law, between liberty and obligation, that the idea of natural right will emerge and be developed. This liberty, natural to man, to which man is obliged by his law, cannot fail to be a natural right of man, a birthright, 'a native right'. It is a right without which the law of nature and the obligation which it imposes would have no meaning. To exist freely is the proper nature of man, the essence which he is obliged to make a concrete reality in his life, and because of this obligation, it is his right.

The natural right of man is then, first of all, 'a right of freedom', a right to freedom: 'freedom of will and liberty of acting' according to the law of nature;[30] freedom from any other power, any other authority, any other will on earth; freedom from all constraint and all violence; freedom to preserve by one's own efforts one's life, one's health, one's liberty, and one's property. Is not freedom the basis, the foundation, of everything else in man?[31] It is clear then that, whereas for Hobbes natural right was concentrated around the preservation and the functioning of 'vital motion', around life, for Locke it is essentially concerned with liberty and its development, its moral, reasonable, concrete realization.

For Hobbes every individual, a self-contained being, strove to preserve himself, with no concern for others. On the other hand, for Locke it is a natural right for every man to develop and defend liberty as such, for others as well as for himself. In reality, it is 'mankind in general', mankind in oneself and in others, that everyone has the right to preserve.[32] He who disobeys the law of nature, that is to say, the law of reason, 'becomes degenerate' in the strict sense of the word: by quitting the principles of human nature, he ceases to belong to human kind, he dehumanizes himself.[33] The right of protecting humanity even in others, is that not truly the human right *par excellence*?

Since the liberty of man, his freedom to act according to his own will, is founded on the fact that he is endowed with reason and that he is capable of 'having reason',[34] everyone equally, each man has, by nature, the right to judge the law of nature. This law is addressed to each man, puts each man under an obligation, from which it follows that each man is its interpreter and judge. We shall not insist on the consequences which Locke draws from this, because he sacrifices them to the advantages of civic life: these consequences are the right of each man to impose on others respect for the law of nature, the right to punish crimes committed against it, and the right to seek reparation for losses suffered.[35] They are, none the less, natural rights and form an integral part of the whole structure. But the important thing here, above all, is this ability and natural right to judge freely for oneself, to be the supreme and absolute authority in judging for oneself.[36] The natural right to freedom of judgement is also the right of not recognizing any authority, unless it be that of reason. Man's freedom finds its principle, its guarantee, and its supreme expression in freedom of judgement, or, what amounts to the same thing, in freedom of judgement subject to the law of reason.

For all that, it must not be thought that Locke confined himself to a purely intellectual conception of natural rights, I mean that he believed that human freedom finds its adequate expression in freedom of judgement. For him, this freedom, and the right to freedom which it proclaims, would be nothing without a concrete and external manifestation, in relation to natural objects and to other men, that is to say, if it did not concern things which can be used and possessed. Property is the external manifestation, the necessary outward expression, of a liberty which has become effective and of a right which is capable of being exercised on things. 'Propriety in the creatures is nothing but that "liberty to use them", which God has permitted.'[37] To say that liberty is a (natural) right, is to say that it can be owned or that it concerns ownership. It follows that there can be no right, no justice, without property. For Locke, that is an ontological truth.[38]

It can also be stated, on the one hand, that man is born with 'a title to perfect freedom and an uncontrolled enjoyment of all the rights and privileges of the law of nature', and on the other hand, that he has 'by nature, a power . . . to preserve his property — that is, his life, liberty, and estate — against the injuries and attempts of other men'.[39] Is not property a title to use and misuse, to have uncontrolled enjoyment of one's possessions? Similarly, in the state of nature, man is free because he is the absolute lord of his own person and possessions.[40] His liberty, is it not an empire? To lose his liberty, is it not to become the property of others? One can understand that, as Locke likes to insist, in these conditions liberty is, together with life, health, and estate, one form of property amongst others.[41]

Consequently the right to property must be considered a 'natural common right'[42] for all men, as following from the law of nature: 'the same law of nature that does . . . give us property, does also bound that property too'.[43] It can be seen that the status of property is of the same type as that of other natural rights. Each man is born with a natural right to the goods he possesses, whatever their quantity;[44] he is even born with the natural right to inherit the property of his ancestors. It is the law of reason, as well as the commandment of God.

There is a sufficient foundation for the right of property in liberty and in the conditions necessary for its effective manifestation; that is why this right exists even in the primitive abundance of the state of nature.[45] The famous theory according to which Locke makes the right to a given property depend on the work performed to gain possession of it or to produce and exploit it, adds no supplementary justification to the theory of the right to property as such. Its aim is to justify the possession of a particular item of property. Each individual, by his work, by the labour of his body and his hands, which are wholly his, mixes what is naturally his own with certain goods of nature to which he has a general, natural right, and he exploits them for the common benefit. In so doing, he makes his goods a part of himself and thereby acquires an exclusive right to them. But for the exclusiveness of this right, others, in gaining possession of his goods, would become owners of his person and his liberty, and this is contrary to natural right.[46]

Locke can then make two deductions from his theory. On the one hand, he can define the limits imposed by natural law on the natural right to property, because 'the measure of property' depends on the possible 'extent of men's labour' as well as on what everyone needs to live.[47] Property is a right to use things, a right tied to the principle that the world has been ordered for the benefit of man. Like liberty, it is a function of human existence: it must help the existence of others and not prevent or interfere with it. On the other hand, Locke gives rules for the elaboration of laws which, in the organization of the State, define property and its use.

There has been a virtuous outcry against this theory, in which the rights of liberty are exercised through property rights (as if it could be otherwise). It would be wiser to note that Locke has used it in a way extremely favourable to the development of the values of liberty and humanity.

Since, in fact, natural rights are applicable only to goods of which one is the owner, it follows that some of them can be alienated; that is to say, that one can renounce the use of them or claims to them, wholly or in part. Far from making the theory of natural right rigid, the theory of property makes it possible to realize and to limit natural rights in civil society by positive laws: Locke shows, in particular, that every property right can be restricted or even suppressed, provided that the interested party consents.

On the contrary, and this is the most significant contribution of Locke to the establishment of a theory of the rights of man, he affirms that, among natural rights, there are some which are the source of all the others, and without the exercise of these an existence which is morally human would no longer be possible: no one then can renounce those rights and claim to alienate them. Locke's reasoning is directly linked with that of Hobbes: it is not in the power of man to renounce his right to life and, *a fortiori*, to transfer to someone else a right which he has not got: 'Nobody can give more power than he has himself.'[48] It is more than a question of physical necessity or of consistency, as with Hobbes; it is a question of nature and of obligation.[49] No one can exempt himself from the obligation to obey the law of nature.[50] No one is within his rights in submitting himself to the arbitrary will of others: this pact is not valid. It is not in the power of man to renounce being what he is, a naturally free being, and to make himself a slave of others. Man has not the liberty to renounce liberty. The slave condition — a state of fact, a state of war, not a state of right — is incompatible with the existence of man and unworthy of it. Because he has failed to fulfil the obligation of his nature, the slave is 'degraded from the common state of rational creatures'.[51] Slavery arises from a 'moral fault'. Failing to be 'a freeman', he is no longer 'a moral man', [52] he is not properly speaking a man. To make use of a term which Locke does not yet employ, but which does no more than indicate his own theory, the natural right to life and to liberty is an inalienable right.

This moreover seems to imply that, in fact, all men do not succeed equally in living a fully human life: Locke recognizes the existence of very different degrees in the human development of individuals. First of all, everything depends on the point of maturity to which they can bring their capacity for reason and their capacity for liberty. Next, everything depends on the moral effort and the work that they put into conquering their human frailty and satisfying the obligations of natural law. But how could it be otherwise if natural law is not a necessity but an obligation? While Locke recognizes that all men are, at birth and by nature, equally capable of liberty and reason, he considers that what people in fact do, and the lives that they in fact lead, are extremely different in value. We would say, today, that if the theory of natural rights starts off by being 'democratic', it ends up by being 'aristocratic', without moreover ceasing in any way to be a theory of natural rights.

In spite of his doctrine of absolute sovereignty, Hobbes, led by the demands of his radical rationalism and his extreme individualism, gave to the doctrine of natural rights (while concentrating narrowly on the human right to life) an incisive form, rich in far-reaching consequences. Locke, no less concerned for reason and the individual, made it the foundation of his liberalism, which was to become Liberalism.

To be sure, this liberalism remains a legal liberalism. It does not go beyond the framework proper to a doctrine of natural rights. It remains formal and abstract, like the rights themselves. In the language of Hegel, Locke is still at the stage of '*Moralität*' and not at the stage of '*Sittlichkeit*'. (Moreover, how could it be otherwise?) He looks on natural rights as legal structures, and not as customs, ways of living, structures of civilization. In the political community, the State guarantees and defends them only in a negative way and by means of law, which is universal and abstract. To enable men effectively to enjoy their natural rights and to allow these rights to serve as a framework for an existence that is free and individual in actual fact, Locke puts his trust in, or rather he relies on, individual effort, on each man's liberty, intelligence, and reason, in short, on his virtue; this alone is capable in his eyes of responding effectively to the obligation of the laws of nature. The only idea which he contemplates is the reciprocal contribution of individuals in educational relationships, which is, in his eyes, the best and indeed the only effective way of ensuring for everyone the full development of reason.

Can we really reproach Locke for stopping in 1690 at a problem which we have not yet solved, and at a solution which we still apply only imperfectly?

For Locke the doctrine of natural rights is identical with the doctrine of Liberalism: one can legitimately wonder if the actual and effective realization of natural rights, which are rights to liberty, by means other than those of law, which are formal and abstract, and those of the individual, which are concrete, does not contradict the idea of individual rights and of liberty. What would be meant by the right and the liberty of a man who was forced to be free, other than a legal right? To condemn Locke is perhaps to condemn Liberalism and the doctrine of the rights of man which is incorporated in it.

(Translated by Sylvia Raphael)

THREE

JOHN W. CHAPMAN

Natural Rights and Justice in Liberalism

DEMOCRATIC in inspiration, ethically demanding, brilliantly analytical, the work of C. B. Macpherson forces one to think again and hard about the unity and the morality of liberalism. The ethic at its heart, he argues, is and has always been 'utilitarian'. Liberal society 'maximizes' at the cost of both justice and freedom. Natural rights are the rights of 'market men', the creatures of market society. Their use creates inequalities both unjust and morally debilitating. As his hand portrays it, 'market society', in its 'possessive' form, is a Hegelian concrete universal, in which the economic, psychological, and ethical components are logically interlocking, hence impervious to reform. Liberalism requires not reformation, for that cannot be had, to the disappointment of John Stuart Mill and T. H. Green; rather reconstruction. 'We need to give up the myth of maximization.'[1]

I do not propose to enter, except incidentally, the controversy over Macpherson's interpretation of the classics. Nor in any direct way do I wish to challenge the historical features of his indictment of liberalism. I shall examine Macpherson's case against the morality of liberal economy on its theoretical merits, and in this I shall rely so far as possible upon his own presentation of the doctrine of natural rights. My purpose is to show that this allows an interpretation other than his own, the significance of which is quite to alter his appraisal of liberalism.

I

Macpherson says that 'a possessive market society is a series of competitive and invasive relations between all men'.[2] That liberal society is 'competitive' is agreed, although surely co-operative and purposive as well. In what sense, or senses, is it to be understood as also 'invasive', something more than merely acquisitive? Hobbes 'was working with a model of society which was essentially contentious'.[3] Moreover, market men are by nature 'contentious and invasive'.[4] Both Hobbes and Locke 'imputed to the nature of society a permanent conflict of interests between individuals. Hobbes's men necessarily sought power over others. Locke's rational men sought unlimited property, which he assumes must be at the expense of others'.[5] Apparently the psychology of market men is 'invasive'. This is so because their character reflects the relations imposed by life in market society, and these are held to be in some objective and non-tautological sense 'invasive'. The argument turns not upon the characteristics attributed to men, for these are the product of their economic and social situation. The relations which obtain in this situation are intrinsically 'invasive', and this is the claim which demands analysis.

In his description of 'possessive market society', Macpherson, on his reading of Hobbes, defines a man's 'powers' to include 'free access' to some land or capital.[6] This definition implies that 'powers' are 'reduced' if a man does not own property. Not only are 'powers' so 'reduced', also to this extent they are 'transferred' to the owner of the land or capital for whom the man works. 'If he can get access, but not freely, his powers are reduced by the price he has to pay for access, and that price measures the amount of his power that is transferred to another.'[7] This means the income of a worker is reduced by the difference between his wage and what he would have earned if he had owned the land or capital he works. This amount now goes to the owner; it is 'transferred' to him; and this 'transfer' defines the 'invasiveness' of the owner-worker relationship.

'Invasiveness' is a composite conceptual innovation, at once ethical and economic. Innovation would be warranted, provided that the new concept clarifies. What Macpherson has really done, however, is to define freedom in terms of power, and produce a definition which carries the implication that an inequality in power is an inequality of freedom. If this inequality is regarded as the outcome of a 'transfer', then it is an 'invasive' inequality; the freedom of one is increased by decreasing the freedom of another. Freedom conceived as power, and power as competitive, together imply that freedom itself is competitive. That such is the liberal conception of freedom is the moral connotation of 'invasiveness'. Certainly economic freedom, or liberty, is rightly considered competitive, but this does not exhaust the liberal conception. Do not natural rights contain also a moral dimension to freedom, one that differs fundamentally from economic freedom in that it is thoroughly non-competitive? Conceptual caution seems the appropriate response to 'invasiveness', as this concept unduly narrows the meaning ascribed to freedom in liberal thought.

From a purely economic standpoint, the difficulty with the concept of 'invasiveness' lies in understanding that the owner-worker arrangement involves a 'transfer'. It does involve an 'inequality'. The real question is whether this inequality is properly viewed as 'invasive'.

Macpherson's models of society present a contrast between a simple market society, the members of which all own property, and so have what he calls 'free access', and the 'possessive' society, in which some own and the others do not. If men are thought of as moving from the former to the latter, it could be contended that there was a 'transfer' of 'powers'. An historical interpretation of 'transfer' is inadequate, however, to support Macpherson's proposition that once possessive society is established the 'transfer' becomes continuous. An economic analysis of the concept is required.

Consider an economy in which returns to capital are taxed from the owners, in part invested, and the remainder distributed in the form of free public services available to all. Assume further that there is full equality of opportunity, unrestricted competition for the position of 'owner', which is now rather that of 'manager', and that both workers and owners receive their marginal value productivity and are compensated for disutility. Their incomes would not be equal, and the differential would reflect not only differences in productivity but also the equalizing increase in real incomes from the free services. This inequality is now seen as being dictated by the requirements of economic rationality. It would hardly seem appropriate to say that it 'measures' a 'transfer' of 'powers'. On the contrary, the 'powers' of both workers and owners have been mutually enhanced; the income inequality performs an allocative function; it is the result of processes which are both competitive and optimizing. To consider such inequalities 'invasive' is misleading, unless all income differentials are to be judged 'invasive' as such. This analysis could be elaborated to take account of income from property to the extent that this form of income offers an incentive essential to optimization and innovation.

If it be held that the relation between worker and owner still includes a difference in 'power', which looks more like authority, and further that this constitutes a 'transfer' of 'power', or a conversion of 'power' into authority, it does not follow that the inequality is inimical to freedom, that one is exploiting the other. Are not owners and workers getting the most out of their respective capacities, given the state of technique and resources? And in this respect their economic freedom does resemble the moral and more collaborative kind. Moreover, the allocation of authority or 'power' is beneficial to both, for it is required to optimize the use of resources. Inequalities there are, both of income and of authority, and these are competitive, although not entirely so. But these inequalities are not meaningfully deemed 'invasive'.

By analysing the morality of economic rationality, my intention is not to contest Macpherson's point that a class system based on private property operates to the disadvantage of the working class. Here wealth, power, and authority all mesh together for the benefit of the classes in which they are concentrated. I should agree in the main that this society is 'invasive', oligopolistic, and unjust in that the material well-being of the few is purchased at the expense of the many, even as, Rousseau would say, the welfare and the moral freedom of all suffer. Class income differentials do not observe criteria of economic efficiency, but obviously partake heavily of monopoly power, which makes possible the imposition of distributive principles inconsistent with both justice and an economic optimum. My analysis is meant to be wholly theoretical and deliberately to abstract from the historical advantages conferred on those who gain or inherit income from property. Useful though the concept of 'invasiveness' may be for the description of class societies, in which economic relations are embedded in social and political institutions, its usefulness would appear to decline directly with the differentiation of economic and political processes, and with elimination of constraints on equality of opportunity, gradual though this is. 'Invasiveness' decreases as a society evolves and becomes more just.

Logically an economic system based on private ownership is no more and no less 'invasive' than one founded on public ownership or one in which property is owned by all. The concept is really historical and political, not economic. Each system would generate income differentials in the cause of economic effectiveness, and there is some reason to think that the pattern of differentials would be pretty much the same, provided that genuine equality of opportunity prevailed to enforce the absence of those non-competing groups known as classes. The quality of authority might well differ significantly, with important consequences for the ethical tone of the societies. If considerations of 'power' are introduced, a full comparative appraisal would have to take account of the interdependences of economic and political power, which will vary with the extent to which societies are advanced, of the ways in which private property disperses as well as concentrates power, and so on. Ultimately ways of life would have to be evaluated in the light of freedom, justice, and welfare; this would include determination of how various forms of inequality may work to offset one another or to advance freedom without infringing the principles of justice.

The composite concept of 'invasiveness', with its assumption that freedom is competitive and its implication that inequality is invidious, obscures rather than clarifies the theoretical, as distinguished from the historical, aspects of comparative analysis. Moreover, Macpherson's concept, used for historical purposes, minimizes the extent to which a market economy, and especially the more advanced, contains not only inequalities but also alternative opportunities, immensely useful for avoiding those forms of personal dependence which liberals find so morally enervating and offensive. As an economy develops, the strategic strength of property declines, and mobility becomes to some degree a substitute for property as the foundation for independence. Freedom differentiates from 'possessiveness'.

II

According to Macpherson, 'invasiveness' comes out in the aggressive attitudes of market men, and it is from this Hobbesian psychology that natural rights are derived. He says 'the reason why Hobbes's natural rights are so different from the traditional ones is that Hobbes was working with a model of society which was essentially contentious, ... in which everyone was always seeking to transfer some of the powers of others to himself'.[8] Hobbes's idea of natural right as placing no obligations on others is analogous to the concept of an economic liberty, or a right of action, and may be passed by to concentrate on Macpherson's exposition of Locke. He thinks Locke's real beliefs about human nature are substantially Hobbes's, and Locke is seen as going beyond Hobbes in the crucial matter of property right.

'If it is labour, a man's absolute property, which justifies appropriation and creates value, the individual right of appropriation overrides any moral claims of the society.'[9] This right, Macpherson holds, is without ethical limitation; the natural right that Locke defends is a right to unlimited property. Perhaps this right is better thought of as an economic liberty, limited in fact by competition, although not in obligation; the justification of such a right would then be tantamount to the defence of an institution or a practice. And, indeed, according to Macpherson, this type of rationale appears to be what Locke had in mind. 'The extended property right is not ... as pure a natural right as the others, for the others do not require any consent. And it is less pure in another respect: it is established by means of utilitarian argument to productivity.'[10] What does it mean to say that a right is 'less pure' than others? The implication is that this right is restricted by 'moral claims of the society'. It calls for specific and distinctive justification. What then is the significance of Locke's asserted 'utilitarian argument to productivity'? If this argument 'establishes' the right, or is the ground, or one of the grounds, of the right, surely the appeal to productivity must also provide constraints on the exercise of the right, or a source of criteria for evaluation of its use.

Macpherson elects to interpret his own analysis of Locke's construction of the natural right to property in the light of the concept of 'invasiveness'. 'Locke, with much ambiguity about the natural contentiousness of men, insisted that they retained an equal right not to be harmed as long as they stayed within the law of nature. He then redefined the law of nature to make it permit unequal access to the means of labour. By doing so, he effectively denied the equal right he had first asserted.'[11] Apparently, in Locke's opinion, no right has been violated, for no one has been 'harmed'. All have gained in comparison with those who work unimproved land. However, Macpherson infers that, although all in this sense may be said to have gained, some are gaining more than others and at the expense of others. There is 'unequal access to the means of labour', hence 'invasion'. Here Macpherson's preoccupation with 'invasiveness' leads him to overlook an alternative analysis of the implications of his own presentation of the property right.

If men have a right not to be 'harmed', and if the practice of appropriation, even the liberty of unlimited appropriation in a competitive context, is to be justified in terms of productivity, the implications are, or rather will become, of consequence. In principle Locke has accepted the optimum conditions implied in the concept of economic rationality! I do not mean, of course, that Locke knows this. The crudeness of his economics is shown in his reference to the American Indian as the relevant standard from which gains are to be reckoned. Placing the Indian properly aside, and noticing only the relations that obtain among the members of the economy, logically Locke may be construed, or rather elaborated, as holding that an inequality is justified only when all directly participating in and affected by the inequality may be expected to gain from it.

As the presence of the Indian reveals, Locke is certainly not calculating in marginal terms; this way of thinking lies in the future. Once maximizing is conceived as equations at various margins, inequalities cannot be rationalized on the ground that the position of all has improved with reference to the irrelevant Indian. Relative, not absolute, gains are relevant, and now differentials must function to maximize, or rather optimize, the allocation and use of resources. Locke invokes productivity in conjunction with his announcement of the principle that all must gain. This demonstrates that he is not advancing a utilitarian principle of justice. Consistently with his belief in natural rights, Locke puts forward a contractarian conception of justice, a conception which implicitly includes the principle that 'inequalities are arbitrary unless it is reasonable to expect that they will work out for everyone's advantage'.[12] Locke's justice is not utilitarian; he does not attempt to argue that the gains for some are so great that they outweigh corresponding losses to others.

A utilitarian theory of justice, that productivity has been enhanced at the price of 'invasiveness', and justly so, can be imputed to Locke only if one finds persuasive Macpherson's concept. In the light of this notion, Locke seems to become either a covert or an unwitting utilitarian, trying to defend inequality, defensible only by a utilitarian theory of justice, with an alternative and incompatible theory, and yet one which is consistent with his theory of rights. May it not be the case that natural rights combined with a marginal version of maximizing productivity have more equalitarian implications than either Locke or Macpherson realizes? Perhaps John Rawls and Abram Bergson,[13] not Jeremy Bentham and A. C. Pigou, are the logical descendants of Locke!

The results of my analysis may be explained in a more abstract manner. Envisage an 'ideal' liberal society from which are excluded all forms of monopolistic and oligopolistic advantage, in which the doctrine of consumers' sovereignty reigns, and there is complete equality of opportunity. Undertake to correct for justice the distribution of income implied by economic rationality. I suggest that one would wish to recover, so far as is practicable, and to redistribute intra-marginal rents — Tawney thought their retention ungentlemanly — and further to provide for special needs and also for needs and values slighted by competitive forces. If he could be persuaded to take account of need, and in a world less harsh than his I see no reason why he should not, could Locke object on principle to this system of production and distribution? It would seem not. For this economy would be consistent with his reference to a standard of productivity in which all share.

Consider now the question: Would the inequalities implicit in this 'ideal' be in any sense 'invasive', that is, unjust? To so hold, having in mind that income and output have been adjusted for needs and rents, would be to imply that the criteria of economic efficiency are sharply, and not merely marginally, incompatible with justice. No doubt, 'the distribution of goods in accordance with merit has a competitive aspect lacking in the case of distribution according to need'.[14] Assuming that competition is not as such unjust, are these inequalities economically rational but not really just? Suppose they reflect not only differences in marginal value productivity but also, as adherence to consumers' sovereignty implies, compensations for marginal disutility. If intra-marginal rent has been extracted and redistributed, as I have assumed, one might well be willing to consider the differentials just, or at least not unjust.

Now imagine an attempt further to equalize incomes. Economic theory suggests that more equalization would hinder optimum allocation of resources, including persons, and would therefore encroach upon the principle of consumers' sovereignty, and hence by implication upon men's rights to make the best of themselves, upon moral freedom to the extent that this is expressed in economic activity. If justice, either separately or in combination with a principle of benevolence, means not merely equal freedom but the greatest equal freedom, the attempt at further equalization would produce injustice. In an 'ideal' liberal society, the principles of justice, the criteria of economic rationality, and the claims of moral freedom may be conceived as theoretically consistent. The natural rights to moral equality and freedom imply a conception of justice, contractarian and not utilitarian, against which rational economic inequality does not offend.

This abstraction is not taken, of course, to portray reality, or even closely to approximate reality. Societies are mixtures of Burkean prejudice and justice. My aim is to design a conceptual alternative to Macpherson's vision of liberalism, to try to show that a liberal society, whatever may have been the historical case, is not as a matter of principle morally defective or incoherent.

For Macpherson, liberalism is a doctrine of economic optimization, implicit in which are a competitive conception of freedom and a utilitarian theory of justice. He recommends that liberalism either be abandoned or overhauled entirely to dispense with those rights and practices which he thinks hinder the achievement of liberal values. Not only should economic efficiency, the 'myth of maximization', be given up, but also the classic liberal conception of human rights, and all this apparently with a view, on a global basis, to 'the generality and rapidity of the transformation from the economy of scarcity to the society of abundance'.[15] I should agree that modern economies produce a good deal of illth and illfare, but the road to abundance, as Marx among others held, goes by way and not in the face of rational economy. Not only welfare but also greater equality and enlarged freedom, for all of which Macpherson calls, may depend on following liberal principles and their more stringent application. 'Equal educational opportunity for all children offers one of the strongest means for lessening inequality of income.'[16] Liberals regard inequalities which do not optimize and serve only to magnify power as both inequitable and dangerous to freedom. Nothing in liberal theory — moral, economic, or political — stipulates their toleration.

III

These reflections on Macpherson's ideas, governed and possibly constricted by liberal theory, may be insufficiently sensitive to the 'potentialities of a mass transformation of human nature'.[17] This possibility invites to psychological and historical investigation upon which one is hesitant to embark. Certainly Rousseau, on the basis of a developmental psychology, saw men as being morally deformed or transformed by society, and Marx, working with a vision of human nature that is both developmental and environmentalist, anticipated even more radical transformations.[18] One wonders how easily Macpherson's use of the concept of 'transformation' may be accommodated to the environmentalism implicit in 'invasiveness'. The former concept is usually found in developmental psychologies such as Rousseau's, whereas the plasticity implied by 'invasiveness' goes with Hobbes and the classical utilitarians. Whether an empirically coherent psychology may be built with both sorts of concepts does seem a question. Marx's psychological assumptions, with which Macpherson seems to agree, feel influenced by the metaphysic of concrete universality, making human nature at once too plastic and also too heavily endowed with potentialities awaiting transformation.

It would be unwise to underestimate human potentialities and premature, to say the least, to attempt to circumscribe them. Perhaps the real question at issue is whether or not liberalism has prevented the release of potentialities, especially those which would be generally recognized as moral and social. Have men become less 'invasive'? Have they acquired a more steady will for justice? Has Rousseau defeated Hobbes, keeping open the question as to Marx's chances against St. Augustine and Freud?

The record is by no means clearly progressive and is certainly far from unblemished. According to Zevedei Barbu, the basic personality structure of the English has altered in a way that differs greatly both from the medieval and the aggressive irrationality exemplified in Hobbes's men. He says 'the English are the first and the most su ccessful among modern nations to create a mental structure in which conscience and instincts are not fundamentally opposed'.[19] This change would seem to be in the direction envisaged as desirable by Rousseau. On the other hand, John Stuart Mill was concerned about the possibility of loss of interest in moral freedom, a concern which is central to much contemporary existentialist thinking. And Barbu himself gives evidence of a literary and projective nature which may suggest 'the end of modern bourgeois personality structure'.[20] Moreover, it is recalled that Rousseau was worried that 'the increase of knowledge has social consequences which strengthen the harmful passions'.[21] Perhaps this fear is offset by D. D. Raphael's observation that 'with the development of the social conscience (and of the economic capacity of a society), the field of justice takes in more from the field of charity'.[22] And on the basis of recent findings, Robert E. Lane surmises: 'In an Age of Affluence, people will come increasingly to trust each other more, to feel more in control of their lives, and to be more hopeful regarding the future. Social alienation will decline.'[23] Perhaps all of these trends and speculations require qualification in the light of Harold D. Lasswell's conclusion, both sombre and promising: 'The culture forms hitherto devised by Homo sapiens are in some profound sense maladapted to his needs. . . . Man suffers from unused capability. . . .'[24]

This review of opinion, brief and tentative, does suggest that there may be change towards the kind of character desired by Macpherson and endorsed by Rousseau, Mill, and Marx. But clearly, as Mill warned, moral advance is highly precarious and difficult to consolidate. There is no reason, however, to think the development of human personality has approximated to any possibly inherent moral limit. Equally there is no reason to believe that liberal society has been retarding psychological evolution.

Does liberalism encourage emulation and also envy to degrees which are fatal for moral freedom and happiness? Not only Hobbes, but also Rousseau and even James Mill were mindful of the moral effects of pride. If men are tempted or driven to let go moral freedom for the sake of disappointing others, liberal society would be condemned as morally repulsive. It seems implausible that people have or will become so materialistic and so anti-social as to find their satisfactions in mutual stultification rather than in the pursuit of 'individual ideals' by all,[25] a quest which is not 'invasive' and promotes the welfare of each. Even inequalities acceptable to justice and which make for freedom would be bitter in a society lacking in a spirit of fraternity, as Rousseau well knew and the principles of '89 proclaim.

IV

If these empirical remarks reinforce, or at least do not contradict, my theoretical analyses, then Macpherson's critique of liberalism comes to this. The classic conceptions of natural law and rights contain, or conceal in a way hitherto unsuspected, a utilitarian theory of justice. It is *'le dieu caché'* of liberalism! For the sake of maximizing productivity, liberalism indulges exploitation. He says 'when tastes changed, as they did in the eighteenth century, the façade of natural law could be removed, by Hume and Bentham, without damage to the strong and well-built utilitarian structure that lay within'.[26] Persistent 'invasiveness' implies that some are profiting on the rest, but this is just in liberal morality, for gains more than balance losses; indeed, there are gains for all by comparison with the 'state of nature'. Bentham's 'principle of utility' only brought to light what had always been hidden in the liberal ethic.

It would be astonishing if a utilitarian conception of justice could be derived from, or combined with, a belief in natural rights, including as these do, in their classic formulation, rights to moral equality and freedom. The derivation is logically impossible, the combination ethically incoherent. How is it that Macpherson comes to think utilitarian conclusions may be reached from contractarian premises? Does liberalism embody a single doctrine, and that utilitarian?

According to Macpherson, 'the equal natural rights Locke envisaged, including as they did the right to unlimited accumulation of property, led logically to differential class rights and so to the justification of a class state. Locke's confusions are the result of honest deduction from a postulate of equal natural rights which contained its own contradiction'.[27] If we put attitudes to one side, and look only at the logic of Locke's argument, his 'confusions' are open to an explanation other than Macpherson's. Not so much 'contradiction' as ambiguity is involved, an ambiguity that depends on Locke's failure fully to appreciate the implications of his defence of inequality in terms of gains in productivity of benefit to all.

He sees that private appropriation improves everyone's absolute position. And Locke may well have been assuming that these gains are greater than could be had if the land were held in individual shares by all. But this assumption would make no difference for his justification, which is that all are gaining. Now assume that it is the case some are gaining more than the others, and this more is at their expense. Still for this state of affairs, Locke offers a defence based upon a contractarian principle of justice, a justification which is flawed but hardly vitiated by his use of an extraneous standard of comparison. Neither does Locke realize that the degree of inequality he confronts could not be rationalized with his productivity criterion once that has been marginally elaborated. It seems to me that together the false standard of comparison and the lack of a concept of optimization make it possible for Locke to accept the situation as consistent with his understanding of justice. The inequality he surveys seems just; natural rights are intact. Later, when Locke's theory of justice becomes allied with marginalism, the paradoxical character of his outlook, apparently at once both contractarian and utilitarian and inconsistently so, is discerned and may be grasped in the light of the principle that any inequality, that is to say, any degree of inequality, in order to qualify as just must optimize.

This analysis shows that Locke does not attempt the logically impossible, the deduction of a teleological and utilitarian theory of justice from a deontological conception of rights. The trouble with Locke is not that his theory of rights contains a 'contradiction' which renders it consistent with a utilitarian, and hence contradictory, theory of justice. This would be to suggest that the unity of liberal doctrine was achieved by way of a double contradiction, first in the theory of rights, and then between theories of rights and justice. The real trouble with Locke is that he is, once the theory of optimization has been worked out, what Herbert Simon would call a 'satisficer', not an 'optimizer'. And Macpherson's difficulty is that he seeks to impose on liberalism a degree of theoretical unity greater than it possesses. His concept of 'possessive market society' attempts to assimilate the logically incompatible contractarian and utilitarian elements in liberal doctrine.

v

As an analytic device, the concept of 'possessive market society' makes insufficient provision for economic, psychological, and intellectual developments. And yet the concept does forcefully direct attention to the ways in which historically considerations of justice appear to have been subordinated to maximizing utility. 'The essentially subordinate status of social justice as a goal of rational political discontent is illustrated by the principle that any group will find it eventually unprofitable to redistribute income toward itself at the cost of even the smallest decline in the rate of economic development.'[28] Here emerges a contrast between the short and the long run, a contrast which is, I think, disconcerting to one's sense of justice. It would seem that some are prepared to sacrifice justice, if not to the requirements of productivity, then to the prospects of development. Is not Macpherson essentially right after all about the morality of liberalism? Is not its ethos fundamentally utilitarian, prepared to trade social justice for economic growth?

Before accepting this conclusion one may wish to consider the possibility that 'initial inequalities in the distribution of offices, rewards, and so on, are required for the promotion of equality in the long run'.[29] The principle suggested here is that we may well be prepared to forgo full justice today for the purpose of a greater justice tomorrow. But this does not imply acceptance of a utilitarian theory of justice. Rather it would seem that our sense of justice recoils from the determination of what might be called the just marginal rate of substitution of justices as between different generations of a society. Perhaps, or more likely probably, our ethical attitudes have not yet become sufficiently precise and integrated to deal with moral questions into which an historical dimension enters. Is it just for the sake of future justice to put up with present injustice, and how much? Notice that it is future justice and not future utility which is at stake. In any event, confidence in one's ethical judgement becomes elusive and fades, and the more so as historical alternatives come into view.

Industrialization on the basis of a class-dominated market society, as Macpherson argues, was swift and brutal; the rates of investment imposed under other circumstances seem even more so. Hobbes was right that international competition would promote economic progress, wrong that it would also guarantee social justice. Is it not also ironical that France which industrialized more slowly and less completely has suffered moral and political consequences which the English have managed to avoid? At this point in history, one is tempted to reflect that no road to modernity is without its moral costs, and one feels driven to comparative evaluations of interdependent imperfections. So much depends on the historical and the political contexts in which a society industrializes, and so much depends upon the relative timing of its industrialization, that questions of justice seem to become absorbed in a general evaluation of the merits, both political and economic, displayed by a system. Theoretical analysis of the sort in which I have engaged becomes submerged in a flow of interdependent events as security competes with justice for the energies of nations. The purpose of analytic effort, however, is not to justify but to understand history and to provide a guide for the present and to the future.

VI

Ultimately a conceptual system must face the test of its capacity to illuminate. In Macpherson's family of analytic concepts that of 'possessive market society' has the look and feel of a concrete universal. It imputes to liberalism a unity appropriate to the analysis of which is the composite concept of 'invasiveness'. The assumption is that liberalism is a unified totality specific to which are interdependences the nature of which may be unlocked only by ideas that ignore conventional theoretical boundaries. And yet 'invasiveness' is not at home in economic theory, is tied to a dubious psychological theory, and hinders understanding of ethical theories. Even its historical virtues tend to disappear in alliance with the master conception of 'possessive market society'. Together they manufacture the illusion that liberalism is a single doctrine of morality to a genetic understanding of which we may attain but which we cannot hope to alter. These conceptual innovations defy the logic of the theoretical distinction between contractarian and utilitarian justice and force upon liberalism a theoretical unity which it does not possess, historically. Lack of historical unity does not imply logical incoherence for liberalism; it is fatal to the metaphysic of concrete universality.

Macpherson's case against liberalism, worthy in many respects of a Rousseau or a Bunyan, deserves admiration and the Scottish verdict: Not proven. The liberal doctrine of natural rights, despite whatever historical disabilities may be attributed to liberalism, still offers a moral foundation for the theoretical reconciliation of the criteria of economic rationality, the claims of moral freedom, and the principles of justice. I see at the core of the doctrine of natural rights the principle that all should benefit, absolutely at least, from inequality in any form; moral equality implies that no one is to gain at the expense of another. One may continue to hope that the principles of efficiency and justice may be institutionalized in ways that release the potentialities and advance the freedom of individuals. Since moral freedom is essentially collaborative rather than competitive, it would seem that so long as men respect one another's individuality and are civil enough not to experience inequalities as 'invasive' the possibility remains open that in a thoroughly liberal society the rational imperatives of justice and economy will be observed. Liberal morality seeks not to go beyond justice, beyond the world of claim and counter-claim, as Bosanquet called it, not because it recognizes no values higher than justice, but because, as W. D. Lamont argued, justice implies respect for persons without which no higher values may be had. The classic doctrine of natural rights implies that justice should prevail for the sake of freedom, and, thanks to C. B. Macpherson, we shall not forget it.

FOUR

MAURICE CRANSTON

Human Rights,
Real and Supposed

IT is said that when that remarkable American jurist Wesley Newcomb Hohfield tried to make the students at Yale Law School discriminate carefully between different uses of the term 'right' in Anglo-American law, he earned himself considerable unpopularity; his pupils even got up a petition to have him removed from his Chair.[1] If the analysis of positive rights is thus resisted by law students we should not be surprised if the analysis of human rights is ill-regarded by many politicians, publicists, and even political theorists. Some politicians, indeed, have a vested interest in keeping talk about human rights as meaningless as possible. For there are those who do not want to see human rights become positive rights by genuine enactments; hence the more nebulous, unrealistic, or absurd the concept of human rights is made out to be, the better such men are pleased.

I shall argue in this paper that a philosophically respectable concept of human rights has been muddied, obscured, and debilitated in recent years by an attempt to incorporate into it specific rights of a different logical category. The traditional human rights are political and civil rights such as the right to life, liberty, and a fair trial. What are now being put forward as universal human rights are social and economic rights, such as the right to unemployment insurance, old-age pensions, medical services, and holidays with pay. I have both a philosophical and a political objection to this. The philosophical objection is that the new theory of human rights does not make sense. The political objection is that the circulation of a confused notion of human rights hinders the effective protection of what are correctly seen as human rights.

One distinction which seems now well established in people's minds is that between human rights or the Rights of Man or natural rights (I take these expressions to mean the same thing) and positive rights, a distinction which corresponds to the distinction between natural law (or justice, or the moral law) and positive law. The distinction has been made better understood by the critics of natural rights, by men like Edmund Burke who could understand what was meant by the rights of Englishmen but not by the Rights of Man, and Jeremy Bentham who said 'Right is the child of law; from real laws come real rights, but from imaginary law, from "laws of nature", come imaginary rights. . . . Natural rights is simple nonsense, natural and imprescriptible rights [an American phrase] rhetorical nonsense, nonsense upon stilts'.[2]

I do not think Bentham's remark is true, but it was worth saying, because it obliges those of us who think natural rights is *not* nonsense to explain what sort of sense it is. For Bentham — and for Burke — the only test of a right was 'Is it actually enjoyed?', 'Is it really enforced?' In other words, 'Is it a positive right?' On this analysis, any right which is not a positive right is not granted the name of a right at all. For Burke the Rights of Man were mere abstractions: the rights of Englishmen were realities — a 'positive recorded hereditary title to all that can be dear to the man and the citizen'.[3] Real rights, again, were positive rights.

Both Burke and Bentham had a political as well as a philosophical interest in this question. Both regarded talk about the Rights of Man as mischievous as well as meaningless. Burke, the conservative, objected to such talk because it stimulated revolutionary sentiments, it injected 'false ideas and vain expectations into men destined to travel the obscure walk of laborious life'. Bentham, the radical, objected to talk about the Rights of Man because it produced declarations and manifestos that had no real significance in positive law, declarations which took the place of effective legislation for the public welfare. Burke disliked the rhetoric that led to public unrest and Bentham disliked the rhetoric that enabled politicians to fob off the public with words instead of deeds. Being thus attacked from Right and Left, it is no wonder that the idea of the Rights of Man, and of Natural Law, became unfashionable in the nineteenth century.

The present century has seen a marked revival of consciousness of what is now generally known as human rights — a term which has the advantage over the older expression 'natural rights' of not committing one too ostentatiously to any traditional doctrine of Natural Law. The reason for this revival is perhaps to be sought in history, first, in the great twentieth-century evils, Nazism, fascism, total war, and racialism, which have all presented a fierce challenge to human rights; and secondly, in an increased belief in, or demand for, equality among men. When the United Nations was set up by the victorious powers in the Second World War, one of the first and most important tasks assigned to it was what Winston Churchill called 'the enthronement of human rights'. The efforts that have been made at the United Nations to fulfil this promise have much to teach a political theorist.

At the inaugural meeting of the Economic and Social Council of the U.N. in May 1946, a Commission on Human Rights was appointed to submit to the General Assembly recommendations and reports regarding an 'International Bill of Rights'. English-speaking delegates on this Commission promptly put forward a draft 'Bill of Rights' in the form of a draft convention or treaty which both named the specific rights to be recognized and provided for the setting up of international institutions to deal with any alleged breach of those rights. The English-speaking delegations not unnaturally interpreted the expression 'Bill of Rights' as meaning an instrument of positive law, and therefore understood the duty of the Commission to be that of finding a formula for making human rights positive rights by making them enforceable. The Russian representative objected to these proposals. He said that it was premature to discuss any measure of a binding or judicial nature; the Soviet Union was willing to support a 'Bill of Rights' only if it was understood as a manifesto or declaration of rights. Some years afterwards the United States followed the Russian example, and announced that it, too, would not commit itself to any legally binding convention for the international protection of human rights.

In the U.N. Commission on Human Rights a compromise was settled on. The Commission agreed first to produce a manifesto or declaration of human rights, and then afterwards begin to work out 'something more legally binding' which it was decided to call a Covenant. The manifesto did not take long to produce. It was given the name of Universal Declaration of Human Rights and proclaimed by the General Assembly of the United Nations in December 1948 (see Appendix, p. 143). The 'more legally binding' Covenant of Human Rights, however, is still, after many years, at the stage of discussion.

One of the difficulties of translating the Universal Declaration of Human Rights into any kind of positive law is that the Declaration contains so much. It has no fewer than thirty articles. The first twenty spell out in detail the sort of rights that were named in the various classical statements of the Rights of Man: the rights to life, liberty, property, equality, justice, and the pursuit of happiness are articulated as, among other things, the right to freedom of movement; the right to own property alone as well as in association with others; the right to marry; the right to equality before the law and to a fair trial if accused of any crime; the right to privacy; the right to religious freedom; the right to free speech and peaceful assembly; the right to asylum. Among the institutions outlawed are slavery, torture, and arbitrary detention.

The Universal Declaration of 1948 did not, however, limit itself to this restatement of the familiar Rights of Man; it includes a further ten articles which name rights of a new and different kind.[4] Article 21 states that everyone has the right to take part in the government of his country, and further articles affirm the right to education; the right to work and to form trade unions; the right to equal pay for equal work; the right of everyone to a standard of living adequate to the health and well-being of himself and his family; the right to security in the event of unemployment, sickness, disability, widowhood, old age, or other lack of livelihood; the right to enjoy the arts and to share in scientific advancement and its benefits; and, what is even more novel, the right to rest, leisure, and 'periodic holidays with pay'.

The difference between these new rights and the traditional natural rights was not unnoticed by those responsible for drafting the Declaration. In the records of the Commission, the first twenty articles are called 'political and civil rights' and the further rights 'economic and social rights'. These later rights appear to have been included under pressure from the Left; but there are many humanitarian people, apart from those on the Left, who (in my belief, unwisely) agree with their inclusion.[5]

So far as the United Nations is concerned, the Commission on Human Rights soon discovered, when it came to draft the 'more legally binding' Covenant, that the two kinds of rights did not mix together well; and the Commission was therefore obliged to draft *two* covenants, one concerning the political and civil rights, the other the social and economic rights. Neither draft has so far proved acceptable to the General Assembly. In the meantime altogether more progress has been made in the field of human rights by another international organization, the Council of Europe. In 1950 a European Convention for the Protection of Human Rights was signed by the member States of the Council of Europe at Strasbourg. This time the so-called 'social and economic rights' were omitted; the rights that were named were the traditional 'political and civil rights'. Moreover, in this case, a European Commission and a European Court of Human Rights were set up with full judicial powers to investigate and remedy any alleged breach of the rights named in the Convention. Here, clearly, is a tangible attempt to translate the human rights into positive rights on an international scale. The only weakness of the European Convention is that some leading European powers, France, Italy, Greece, and Turkey, have refused to recognize the jurisdiction of the European Court or to grant the right to individual petition to the Commission or the Court. Nevertheless a dozen other nations *do* recognize these institutions; so that changes in positive law have helped in those places to make men's 'human rights' positive rights.[6]

One of the objections to regarding the 'social and economic' rights as authentic human rights is that it would be totally impossible to translate them in the same way into positive rights by analogous political and legal action. There are other objections: but the time has now come to consider more carefully what is meant by a right, and then what kind of right a human right is. We have already noted the distinction between human rights and positive rights; I propose now to rearrange rights into two other categories; the one I shall call legal rights, the other moral rights.

(1) LEGAL RIGHTS may be distinguished as follows:

(*a*) *General positive rights:* the rights that are enjoyed and fully assured to everyone living under a given jurisdiction or constitution.

(*b*) *Traditional rights and liberties:* Burke said that the English people had risen against James II because he had taken away their traditional rights and liberties as Englishmen. The Vichy government took away many of the traditional rights and liberties of Frenchmen. This class of rights includes lost positive rights as well as existing positive rights.

(*c*) *Nominal 'legal' rights*: Even the least liberal nations tend to have 'façade' constitutions[7] which 'guarantee' freedom of speech, movement, assembly, and other such rights to their inhabitants. But where these nominal rights are not enforced, they cannot, of course, be classed as positive rights. We nevertheless see the demand in some such places for the nominal 'legal' rights being made positive rights. One example is the demand of certain Polish intellectuals for that freedom of expression which their constitution assures them. An even more publicized example is the demand of the Negroes in the United States for the nominal legal right to vote, enter State schools, and so forth, to be translated into positive rights.

(*d*) *Positive rights, liberties, privileges, and immunities of a limited class of persons*: Under this category we should have to include all rights which are attached to membership of a given category, e.g., the rights of clergymen, of peers, of doctors, of graduates of the University of Oxford, and of freemen of the City of London. The twentieth century has become impatient of privileges, and rights which were once enjoyed by a limited class of persons are often now claimed by all the inhabitants of a country. For example, the privileges of citizenship, the rights of ratepayers, as they were known in nineteenth-century England, are now enjoyed by all adult British subjects. A demand for the extension of rights within a political society is often confused with the demand for human rights. But the two are quite distinct.

(*e*) *The positive rights, liberties, privileges, and immunities of a single person*: Here the examples are few, because the cases are few: the rights of the President of the United States, of the Chairman of the Senate; the rights of the King, or the Lord Chancellor, or the Archbishop of Canterbury, are examples. Since the decay of the doctrine of the Divine Right of Kings, this class of rights does not present much of a problem.

The foregoing classes cover the category of legal rights. Next in turn is the category of moral rights. In this case it will be convenient to reverse the order of generality.

(2) MORAL RIGHTS

(*a*) *Moral rights of one person only:* We remember Bradley's famous phrase 'my station and its duties': we can equally speak of 'my station and its rights'. I, and I alone, have a network of rights which arise from the fact that I have done certain deeds, paid certain monies, been elected to certain places, and so forth. Some of these rights are legal rights as well as moral rights. But in considering them as moral rights the question is not 'Does the law uphold them?' but 'Have I just claim to them?' Not all my moral rights may in fact be enjoyed. Often we become most conscious of our moral rights precisely when they are *not* upheld. I am inclined to say 'I have a moral right to be told what is going on in my own house' when I realize I am not being told. So just as the crucial question with legal rights is 'Are they secured and enjoyed?', the crucial question in a moral right is 'Is there a just title?' Is there a sound moral claim? *Justification* is the central question.

(*b*) *The moral rights of anyone in a particular situation:* This is the class of moral rights which belongs to everyone who comes into a certain specific category, e.g., that of a parent, or a tutor, or an *au pair* girl. So we can say of a person, if he is a member of this class, he is entitled to so and so. Claims to have such moral rights are pressed by proving that one does belong to the appropriate category.

(*c*) *The moral rights of all people in all situations:* Because these rights are universal we should naturally expect them to be few in number; and we should expect them to be highly generalized in their formulation. It is easier to agree, for example, about the kind of deed which violates the right to life than it is to agree about any philosophical expression of the right to life. Moreover, it is inevitable that such a right as that to liberty will be somewhat differently understood in different societies, where the boundary between liberty and licence will be differently drawn. Again, our understanding of the right to property will differ according to the meaning we give to that richly ambiguous word.

The place which human rights occupy in my classification is readily understood. Human rights are a form of moral right, and they differ from other moral rights in being the rights of all people at all times and in all situations. This characteristic of human rights is recognized in the first paragraph of the preamble to the Universal Declaration of 1948, which says: 'Whereas recognition of the inherent dignity and of the equal and inalienable rights of all members of the human family is the foundation of freedom, justice and peace in the world. . . .'

Part of the difficulty of justifying human rights is their very universality. Moral rights of classes (2) (*a*) and (2) (*b*) above are justified by reference to the definite station or situation of the claimants. I claim a right to be told about the health of Nicholas Cranston by showing that I am his father. I do not think anyone else (except his mother) has the same right. But human rights do not depend in any way on the station or the situation of the individual. This is part of what is meant by saying they are 'rights that pertain to a human being merely because he is a human being'. If the validity of a moral right is commonly established by reference to the station or situation of the claimant, it is not altogether easy to see by what tests one could validate the rights which are *not* considered in relation to any definite situation.

Nevertheless there are some tests for the authenticity of a human right or universal moral right. Rights bear a clear relationship to duties. And the first test of both is that of practicability. It is not my duty to do what it is physically impossible for me to do. You cannot reasonably say it was my duty to have jumped into the Thames at Richmond to rescue a drowning child if I was nowhere near Richmond at the time the child was drowning. What is true of duties is equally true of rights. If it is impossible for a thing to be done, it is absurd to claim it as a right. At present it is utterly impossible, and will be for a long time yet, to provide 'holidays with pay' for everybody in the world. For millions of people who live in those parts of Asia, Africa, and South America where industrialization has hardly begun, such claims are vain and idle.

The traditional 'political and civil rights' can (as I have said) be readily secured by legislation; and generally they can be secured by fairly simple legislation. Since those rights are for the most part rights against government interference with a man's activities, a large part of the legislation needed has to do no more than restrain the government's own executive arm. This is no longer the case when we turn to 'the right to work', 'the right to social security', and so forth. For a government to provide social security it needs to do more than make laws; it has to have access to great capital wealth, and many governments in the world today are still poor. The government of India, for example, simply cannot command the resources that would guarantee each one of the 480 million inhabitants of India 'a standard of living adequate for the health and well-being of himself and his family', let alone 'holidays with pay'.

Another test of a human right is that it shall be a genuinely universal moral right. This the so-called human right to holidays with pay plainly cannot pass. For it is a right that is necessarily limited to those persons who are *paid* in any case, that is to say, to the *employé* class. Since not everyone belongs to this class, the right cannot be a universal right, a right which, in the terminology of the Universal Declaration, 'everyone' has. That the right to a holiday with pay is for many people a real moral right, I would not for one moment deny. But it is a right which falls into section (2) (*b*) of the classification of rights which I have set out above; that is, a right which can be claimed by members of a specific class of persons *because* they are members of that class.

A further test of a human right, or universal moral right, is the test of *paramount importance*. Here the distinction is less definite, but no less crucial. And here again there is a parallel between rights and duties. It is a paramount duty to relieve great distress, as it is not a paramount duty to give pleasure. It would have been my duty to rescue the drowning child at Richmond if I had been there at the time; but it is not, in the same sense, my duty to give Christmas presents to the children of my neighbours. This difference is obscured in the crude utilitarian philosophy which analyses moral goodness in terms of the greatest happiness of the greatest number: but common sense does not ignore it. Common sense knows that fire engines and ambulances are essential services, whereas fun fairs and holiday camps are not. Liberality and kindness are reckoned moral virtues; but they are not moral duties in the sense that the obligation to rescue a drowning child is a moral duty.

It is worth considering the circumstances in which ordinary people find themselves invoking the language of human rights. I suggest they are situations like these:

A black student in South Africa is awarded a scholarship to Oxford, and then refused a passport by the South African government simply because he is black. We feel this is clear invasion of the human right to freedom of movement.

Jews are annihilated by the Nazi government, simply because they are Jews. We feel this is a manifest abuse (an atrocious abuse) of the human right to life.

In several countries men are held in prison indefinitely without trial. We feel this is a gross invasion of the human right to liberty and to a fair trial on any criminal charge.

In considering cases of this kind, we are confronted by matters which belong to a totally different moral dimension from questions of social security and holidays with pay. A human right is something of which no one may be deprived without a grave affront to justice. There are certain deeds which should never be done, certain freedoms which should never be invaded, some things which are supremely sacred. If a Declaration of Human Rights is what it purports to be, a declaration of universal moral rights, it should be confined to this sphere of discourse. If rights of another class are introduced, the effect may even be to bring the whole concept of human rights into disrepute. 'It would be a splendid thing', people might say, 'for everyone to have holidays with pay, a splendid thing for everyone to have social security, a splendid thing to have equality before the law, and freedom of speech, and the right to life. One day, perhaps, this beautiful ideal may be realized. . . .'

Thus the effect of a Universal Declaration which is overloaded with affirmations of so-called human rights which are not human rights at all is to push *all* talk of human rights out of the clear realm of the morally compelling into the twilight world of utopian aspiration. In the Universal Declaration of 1948 there indeed occurs the phrase a' common standard of achievement' which brands that Declaration as an attempt to translate rights into ideals. And however else one might choose to define moral rights, they are plainly *not* ideals or aspirations.

Rights have been variously defined by jurists and philosophers. Some have spoken of them in terms of 'justifiable claims' or 'moral titles'; others have analysed rights in terms of duty ('what we have an overwhelming duty to respect'); others again have preferred to speak of right conduct or obligation or of ought ('a man has a right whenever other men ought not to prevent his doing what he wants or refuse him some service he asks for or needs'). All these words — 'right', 'justice', 'duty', 'ought', 'obligation' — are the key terms of what Kant called the 'categorical imperative'. What ought to be done, what is obligatory, what is right, what is duty, what is just, is not what it would be nice to see done one day; it is what is demanded by the basic norms of morality or justice.

An ideal is something one can aim at, but cannot by definition immediately realize. A right, on the contrary, is something that can, and from the moral point of view *must*, be respected here and now. If this were not so, we should have to agree with Bentham; if the Rights of Man were ideals, to talk of them as rights at all would indeed be rhetorical nonsense. We can give sense to human rights only because we can reasonably claim that men have moral rights, and that among the moral rights which each man has are some that he shares with all other men.

To deny that the 'economic and social rights' are the universal moral rights of all men is not to deny that they may be the moral rights of some men. In the moral criticism of legal rights, it is certainly arguable that the privileges of some members of a certain community ought to be extended to other members (and perhaps all members) of that community. But this matter is correctly seen as a problem of *socialization* or *democratization* — that is, the extension of privileges and immunities — rather than as a problem about the universal rights of all men: and the case for any such specific claims to an extension of legal rights must be argued on other grounds.

FIVE

D. D. RAPHAEL

Human Rights, Old and New

THE concept of Human Rights, as they are called in the English text of the Universal Declaration of 1948, is of course a revival of the eighteenth-century concept of the Rights of Man. According to Mrs. Eleanor Roosevelt, who was Chairman of the United Nations Commission on Human Rights, the old phrase was changed because of an interpretation given to it, at an early stage of international discussion, by a delegate from some benighted country. 'I assume', he blandly remarked, 'that when we speak of the rights of man, we mean what we say. My government, of course, could not agree to extend these rights to women.' The French text of the Universal Declaration retains the traditional '*droits de l'homme*', perhaps because the French can count on a general appreciation of legal as of other niceties concerning the relations between the sexes, and are familiar with the dictum that, in the language of the law, 'the male is presumed to embrace the female'.

In the eighteenth century, when there was no place for Mary Wollstonecraft on an official commission, it was not thought necessary to express the universality of these moral rights by the adjective 'human'. But in order to show that their moral force is independent of positive law, they were described by more pompous adjectives — 'natural', 'inherent', 'inalienable', 'imprescriptible' — that were to be deflated by Bentham in a well-known jibe (already quoted by Mr. Cranston): 'Natural rights is simple nonsense, natural and imprescriptible rights rhetorical nonsense, nonsense upon stilts.' Let us lay aside the stilts and look at the 'simple nonsense' as it first showed itself in the history of political theory. The notion of Natural Rights finds its chief expression in Locke and is a development from the theory of Natural Law.

The traditional doctrine of natural law does not give any particular prominence to the idea of individual rights. Law implies both duties and rights, and it is no doubt fair to say that the ancient and medieval theories of natural law were more concerned with the foundations of moral, legal, and political duty than with the foundations of rights. Nevertheless, Hobbes is quite wrong when he says that traditional theorists have confused '*jus* and *lex*, *right* and *law*' (*Leviathan*, Ch. 14). In English we do not speak of a system of right, as we speak of a system of law, but Latin and various modern European languages find it natural to use the noun 'right' as more or less synonymous with 'law' when referring to a legal system as a whole. Consequently the expression '*ius naturale*' means the system of natural law. The reason for this usage is that a system of law is at one and the same time a system of duties and a system of rights. For example, a law which requires *A* to fulfil his contract with *B*, or a law which forbids *A* to assault *B*, lays a duty on *A* and confers a right on *B*. Indeed, this last clause is just saying the same thing in two different ways. The statement, '*A* has a duty to fulfil his contract to *B*', means the same as the statement, '*B* has a right against *A* to the fulfilment of his contract'; and the statement, '*A* has a duty to refrain from assaulting *B*', means the same as the statement, '*B* has a right against *A* to freedom from assault'. Consequently, a system of law, 'natural' or positive, is a set of rules which may be regarded either as listing duties which men have towards each other, or as listing rights which they have against each other. And since positive law in fact tends to begin from the notion of rights to be protected, it is intelligible that such a set of rules should be called a system of *ius* (or *droit*, etc.) more readily than it is called a system of *lex* (or *loi*, etc.).

The fact is that the meanings which Hobbes gives, both to natural law and to natural right, are radically different from the meanings which these terms have in the traditional doctrine and which they retain in Locke. By 'radically different' I mean not only different in content but different in conception. It is often said, for example, that Hobbes, like Locke, holds that there is a natural right to life. This is a mistake — but not on the ground that Hobbes gives a different content to a right of the same character. According to Hobbes, every man will inevitably endeavour to preserve his life; his natural right is to do whatever he thinks is a means to this inevitable aim of self-preservation. Natural right for Hobbes is a right *to act*, it is not a right *to have* something or a right *against* other persons. Again, natural law, according to Locke and earlier tradition, lays down duties which largely consist of duties *towards* others. According to Hobbes, however, the requirements of natural law are not duties to others.

We speak of 'a right' in two different senses. The first sense I call a right of action (not to be confused with a technical use of this term in the law). Here we speak of a right to do something. Such a right is equivalent to an absence of obligation. If *A* has a right to sing in his bath, to cultivate his garden, or to give away his inheritance, this means that he has no obligation to refrain from these actions. In doing such an action, he is doing nothing wrong. He is morally and legally free to do the action, i.e., he is not morally or legally bound to refrain. This is how Hobbes uses the term 'natural right'; it is, as Hobbes calls it, a liberty, a freedom from the impediment of obligation imposed by any law.

The second sense of 'a right' I call a right of recipience. Here we speak of a right against someone else, i.e., a right to receive something from him, even if the something is simply the facility of being left alone. Such a right is equivalent to the existence of an obligation on the part of the other person against whom one has the right. If *A* has a right against *B* to have a contract fulfilled or a debt paid, this means that *B* has an obligation to *A* to fulfil the contract or pay the debt. And if *A* has a right to be left free from interference by *B*, this means that *B* has an obligation to *A* to leave him alone. A right to be left alone is a right *to liberty*, i.e., a right to freedom from interference by other people; but this should not be confused with a right of action, which can itself be called *a liberty*, i.e., a freedom from obligation.

E. F. Carritt (*Ethical and Political Thinking*, p. 77) denied this distinction on the ground that a right to act is simply a right to freedom from interference with one's action, and so is what I call a right of recipience. In my view, a man who has a right of action, a freedom from obligation, has *in addition* a right of recipience to freedom from interference. To say that he has the first right is to say that his proposed action is itself not wrong or unlawful, and it is only when this is true that he has the second right to freedom from interference. The second right depends on the first, but not *vice versa*. It seems at first sight plausible to deny that the first, the right of action, exists independently, because people do not normally speak of their rights of action unless someone else hinders them or at least interferes to the extent of querying the propriety of their action. If Lewis Carroll's Father William were not only incessantly to stand on his head, but were incessantly to declare that he had a right to do it, he would be called senile, not just old. He justifies his acrobatics only when the youth queries whether, at his age, it is right. Thus it seems sensible to say that one who speaks of his right to act is telling others that they have no business to interfere. But consider the meaning of a statement denying a right to act. Suppose Father William were to kick his son downstairs without the provocation that he receives in the poem, and suppose a spectator were to say, 'You have no right to kick the boy'. According to Carritt, a statement that a man has no right to act means simply that 'nobody has the duty not to prevent him'. Our spectator, then, would mean only that he and others were not obliged to stand by while Father William did his kicking, i.e., that their interference would not be wrong. But this is too weak to express the force of the spectator's statement, which means that something else, the action of Father William himself, is quite definitely wrong.

In the traditional doctrine of natural law, rights are rights of recipience, rights against other people. These rights correspond to, or rather they are simply another way of looking at, the duties of those other people to the persons who are said to have the rights. The rights are rights against other people, and the duties are duties to other people. Thus a system of natural law, a system of duties which all men have to others, is at the same time a system of rights which all men have against others.

The traditional doctrine of natural law, when speaking of duties, does not in fact confine them to duties towards other men. Theological versions of the doctrine usually refer to three categories of duty: duty to God, duty to self, and duty to other men. Exponents of the doctrine in this form might go on to say that ultimately all duties are duties to God; duties to self and duties to other men are ultimately duties to God because all men are created by God and belong to God. However, in so far as men have rights against each other, these rights correspond to their duties to each other.

In the theory of Hobbes, on the other hand, the obligations of
natural law are not obligations to other men. For one who believes that
the laws of nature are commands of God, the obligations imposed by
natural law are obligations to God. But both for the believer and for the
atheist, the so-called laws of nature are rules for self-preservation, i.e.,
maxims of prudence. One could say that they are therefore duties to
self (and ultimately, for the believer, duties to God), but they are not
duties to other men. Consequently they do not correspond to rights of
recipience held by other men. There are no *natural* rights of recipience
in Hobbes's theory. Rights of recipience for Hobbes (though Hobbes
does not call them 'rights' — he speaks of what is 'due'), and likewise
obligations to other men, are artificial, not natural. If *A* makes a
promise to *B*, *A* thereby imposes upon himself an artificial obligation,
an obligation *towards B*, and this is tantamount to saying that he sets
up an artificial right for *B*, a right of recipience against *A* himself.
Since there are no natural rights of recipience, Hobbes has to give a
different interpretation to the notion of natural right. For him, natural
right is right of action, the absence of obligation. That is why he
opposes natural right and natural law.

Locke is not altogether consistent in his usage, but on the whole he
follows the tradition. The obligations of natural law include obligations to other men, and therefore natural rights are, by and large, rights
of recipience against other men. My natural right to life is a right
against other men that they should not deprive me of my life; it
corresponds to their natural obligation not to kill me. My natural right
to liberty is a right against other men that they should leave me in
peace; it corresponds to their natural obligation to leave me in peace.
My natural right to 'estate' (property in the narrower sense of the
word) is, I think, a mixture of right of action and right of recipience.
On the one hand, I am, in certain conditions, free from obligation to
leave land and its products available for common use; I have a right of
action, a right to consume and appropriate. On the other hand, appropriation is not just simple action; it implies a right of recipience. When
I fence in a piece of land with which I have 'mixed my labour', I
thereby declare that I *alone* have the right to use it; this implies that
others have an obligation not to use it, i.e., I have a right of recipience
that they should keep out.

Hobbes's idea of natural right is an aberration from the tradition that led to the concept of human rights. Human rights are rights of recipience, not rights of action. Some of the rights in the Universal Declaration are framed in a way that perhaps suggests rights of action. For example, Article 14 speaks of a right *to seek* asylum from persecution, Article 21 of a right *to take part* in government, and Article 23 of a right *to work*. But of course the meaning of these Articles is not that it is morally permissible for a man to seek asylum from persecution, to participate in government, or to work. Nobody needs to be told that. When the American Declaration of Independence spoke of a natural right to pursue happiness, it was not arguing against ascetics and kill-joys that there was nothing wrong in pursuing happiness. And when Louis Blanc enunciated a right to work, he was not arguing against any advocates of the virtues of idleness. All these rights are rights of recipience. The right to pursue happiness, and the right to seek asylum, are claims *to be allowed* to do these things. Likewise, the right to work, and the right to participate in government, are claims *to be given the opportunity* for work and for political activity.

Someone may say that here at least there is no real difference between a right of action and a right of recipience. It would indeed be silly to understand Article 14, for example, as a statement that it *is morally* permissible to seek asylum from persecution; but it is not silly to understand the Article as a statement that it *ought* to be *legally* permissible to seek asylum from persecution. Therefore, the objector may say, the Article enunciates a right of action in the sense of a liberty that ought to be allowed by law. Similarly the right to pursue happiness, in the American Declaration, may be interpreted as a claim that individuals ought to be legally free to pursue happiness.

This objection is misplaced, for two reasons. First, the statement that it *ought* to be legally permissible for any man to seek asylum from persecution means that governments have a moral obligation to their subjects to make this legally permissible; and to say that governments have a moral obligation to their subjects is the same as saying that the subjects have a moral right against the governments. Consequently the objector has admitted that Article 14 of the Universal Declaration is a statement that everybody has a *recipient* right to be permitted by law to seek asylum. A right to be allowed to act (as distinct from a right to act) is a right of recipience, because it corresponds to an obligation on the part of other people to refrain from interference when one exercises a right of action. It is a right *to liberty*, whereas the right of action itself is *a liberty*.

The second reason why the objection is misplaced is that certain of the rights under discussion are rights to more than liberty, so that the proposed identification with rights of action as liberties does not apply to them anyway. The right to seek asylum and the right to pursue happiness are recipient rights to liberty, claims to be simply left free or allowed by law to do what one wants to do. But the other two examples mentioned earlier are different. Take first the right to participate in government. Is this simply a claim to be *allowed* by law to participate? To be sure, it is not a claim to be *required* to vote, still less to be *required* to stand for election! But it is not simply a claim for a liberty either; it is a claim for an opportunity. There is no point in urging that the laws should not forbid me to vote or to stand for election, unless the laws also make positive provision for people to vote and to stand for election. The difference is even plainer with the right to work. A declaration of a right to work would be silly, not only if it meant that there was nothing wrong in working, but also if it meant that there should be no law forbidding work. To speak of a right to work is to claim that a positive opportunity to work should be provided.

It is therefore a mistake to think that some human rights are rights of action and others rights of recipience. What I have just said about liberties and opportunities, however, points to a real and important difference among human rights. Some are rights to liberty, rights to be *allowed* something, while others are rights to opportunity or more than opportunity, rights to be *given* something. We come here to the distinction between the older concept of Civil Rights (or Rights of Liberty) and the relatively more recent concepts of Political, Economic, and Social Rights. When a man has a right to liberty, the obligation of those against whom he has the right is a *negative* obligation, an obligation to leave him alone, to leave him free to do as he thinks fit. But when he is said to have a right to participate in government, or a right to work, and even more when he is said to have a right to social security, the obligation of those against whom he has the right is a *positive* obligation, an obligation to provide him with something which he could not achieve by himself. When we say, for example, that a man has the right to participate in government, we mean that those who organize the political life of the country are obliged to give him the opportunity to vote and make his opinions known, and that they are further obliged to have regard to his opinions when they take their political decisions. The right to work means that the government has a duty to prevent unemployment so far as it can. The right to social security means that the community as a whole has a duty to provide its needy members with the means of subsistence and with essential services such as schools and hospitals.

Locke summed up the content of his concept of natural rights as a right to property, giving the word 'property' an extended meaning so as to cover life and liberty as well as 'estate'. He had his own reasons for this peculiar usage. It would be more appropriate to pick out the word 'liberty' as a compendious term to cover the content of Locke's three natural rights to life, liberty, and property. In Locke's conception, natural right is a right to be left free to live (or, if one is unlucky, to die), to be left free to do as one chooses, and to be left free to enjoy the fruits of one's labour.

Mr. Maurice Cranston, writing on p. 46 of the preceding essay about economic and social rights as 'rights of a new and different kind', includes among them the right to take part in the government of one's country (a right which I have preferred to call political). Earlier, in his book, *Human Rights Today*, p. 38, he said, rather incautiously, that 'economic and social rights were unknown to Locke and the natural rights theorists of the eighteenth century', and there too (on p. 37) he coupled the political right to participate in government with economic and social rights, all of these being contrasted with the older conception of 'civil rights' or rights of liberty. He would probably now agree that his generalization about the *eighteenth* century needs to be qualified. Locke certainly confined himself to rights of liberty (life, liberty, and property); and 'the pursuit of happiness', which the American Declaration of Independence substituted for 'property', is still a right of liberty. It might be said also that the addition of 'security', in the Virginian Declaration of Rights, and in the French Declaration of 1789, does not substantially change the conception of rights of liberty or civil rights. Both these declarations, however, go on to speak of the political right to take part in government by way of voting for representatives. Nor is this all. There are also suggestions, even in the eighteenth century, of what are now called economic and social rights. Mr. Cranston has referred, in note 4 of the preceding essay, to an article by Professor Carl J. Friedrich ('Rights, Liberties, Freedoms: A Reappraisal', *American Political Science Review*, lvii, Dec. 1963), drawing attention (p. 843) to statements, by Turgot in 1776 and by Robespierre in 1793, of a right to work, and, in the French Declaration of 1793, of a right to education. So far as France is concerned, we may add the *Manifeste des Égaux* of the Babeuf Conspiracy of 1796, which spoke of a universal right to education (and a universal obligation to work). In one of the English theorists of the time, furthermore, there is a far more detailed conception of what we now call economic and social rights. Thomas Paine, in Part I of *The Rights of Man* (1791), enunciates and discusses the general principles of the French Revolutionaries; but in Chapter 5 of Part II (1792), he applies these principles in a carefully thought-out plan of what we should now call social security. It included, for all who needed them, a State system of education, children's allowances, old-age pensions, maternity, marriage, and funeral allowances, and a scheme of publicly endowed employment for the poor of London. In *Agrarian Justice* (1797), he sets out a revised plan, with a different method of financing a simpler system of benefits, available this time to all, whether rich or poor. He says emphatically, in both works, that he is speaking of a right and not of charity.

Of course all these suggestions of economic and social rights come towards the end of the eighteenth century and are pointers to socialist theory of the nineteenth century, though only one of the men so far mentioned, Babeuf, could be called in any sense a socialist. In general it is true that the advocates of the rights of man in the eighteenth century thought chiefly, like Locke, of civil rights or rights of liberty, rights to be left in peace by other men and by governments except in so far as governments were fulfilling their task of keeping the peace and preserving men's liberties. The functions of government were regarded by most men at that time as negative functions, to protect individuals in the enjoyment of what they already possessed, and to leave them free to fend for themselves so long as they did not encroach upon the established legal rights of others. The idea that a government also has the positive duties of increasing welfare and of redistributing wealth more justly is a product mainly of nineteenth-century socialist thought. In so far as this idea of the positive duties of government was expressed under the notion of rights, of the just claims of need, it owes most to French theorists of the period, especially Louis Blanc and Proudhon.

Mr. Cranston argues that it is a mistake to class economic and social rights with the older 'natural' rights of liberty. Human rights, he says on pp. 49–51 of his essay, are universal moral rights, and in addition to being genuinely universal they must satisfy two further tests, of practicability and of paramount importance. I agree with Mr. Cranston that these are appropriate tests, but they do not in fact draw a clear line between the earlier and the later concepts of human rights. Tom Paine evidently understood the natural right to life as implying not only laws against homicide but also laws to provide a bare subsistence. Will anyone say that he was wrong in terms of paramount importance? Nobody would accept Clough's satirical couplet:

> 'Thou shalt not kill, but need'st not strive
> Officiously to keep alive.'

Importance, like practicability, is of course a matter of degree, and no doubt the prevention of murder is of more paramount importance than the prevention of starvation. Yet the degrees of paramountcy do not place all the rights of liberty before all the economic and social rights. If a man is subject to chronic unemployment in a depressed area, he will not thank you for the information that he has the basic rights of liberty. Locke's right of freedom to amass property is of little interest to such a man when it goes along with 'freedom to starve'. J. S. Mill's plea for absolute freedom of expression cuts little ice with labourers who do not know whether they will have a job next month.

I have not forgotten practicability. Tom Paine's plan for social security was eminently practicable for the England of his day, as he took care to show, but even his modest scheme would not be feasible universally. Yet this is not to say that poorer nations are unable to organize any aid at all for the needy; a sort of system of social security is to be found in the Old Testament laws about leaving harvest gleanings for the poor, the periodic cancellation of debts, and so forth. Again, while unemployment is among the greatest of evils for those

who are subject to it, no amount of reading Lord Keynes will produce
a golden key for full employment everywhere. Yet there is some
possibility nowadays of some control of unemployment by governments,
as there was not in former times, and therefore it is justifiable to speak
of a duty of governments to do what they can. After all, no amount of
criminal legislation or of police forces will be able to prevent *all*
homicides; but that is no reason for saying that the right to life must be
struck out of our list of human rights as not being universally practicable. Nobody suggests that the right to work or the right to social
security can be implemented to the same degree everywhere. Article
22 of the Universal Declaration, in introducing economic and social
rights, recognizes that the entitlement has to be 'in accordance with the
organization and resources of each State'.

Mr. Cranston justifiably derides the extravagance of Article 24 in
calling holidays with pay a universal right. But we could also deride the
extravagance of Article 19 in speaking, without any reservations, of a
universal right to seek, receive, and impart information through any
media and regardless of frontiers. On the face of it, this Article would
justify the transmission to a foreign power of secret military information, the tapping of telephone conversations, the opening of private
correspondence, or the prying by any newspaper reporter into the
private lives of individuals. Of course the Article does not in fact intend
these consequences. It needs to be read in conjunction with Article 12,
which forbids arbitrary intrusion upon privacy, and with Article 30,
which limits the exercise of any right so as not to aim at the destruction
of other rights. Likewise Article 24, with its provision for holidays
with pay, needs to be read in the light of Article 22, which sets a
general limit on economic and social rights so as to accord with the
resources of each State. I should agree, nevertheless, that the inclusion
of holidays with pay is an absurd extravagance. It is so, however, not
because the alleged universal right to holidays with pay is an economic
or social right, but because holidays with pay are a luxury. The general
principle of Article 24, the right to rest and leisure, is a perfectly
proper element in a list of basic rights and duties. If I may refer to the
Old Testament again, the Mosaic Decalogue included a day of rest
along with the prohibition of elementary crimes like murder and theft.
To the manual worker (and that means to two-thirds of the working

population even in advanced societies), some security of employment and a reasonable limitation of working hours mean more than certain (I do not say all) parts of the classical rights of liberty.

I have said that the inclusion of holidays with pay is an extravagance because holidays with pay are a luxury. To call something a right (of recipience) is to say that it is morally necessary. A luxury is an enjoyment that goes beyond necessity. There is, however, no fixed principle for drawing the line between those wants that are regarded as 'needs' (a species of moral necessity) and those that are not. Ideas of what is due as a matter of moral necessity for human personality vary from one age to another and from one society to another. In general, material and moral progress produces a continuous expansion of the conception of needs. It is therefore to be expected that a twentieth-century declaration of rights should include more than an eighteenth-century declaration, and what is thought to be a luxury today may be regarded as a necessity tomorrow.

I have argued that Mr. Cranston's tests of practicability and paramount importance do not afford a criterion for distinguishing the rights of liberty from economic and social rights. There is a sense, however, in which it is correct to say that the rights of liberty are universal moral rights while political, economic, and social rights are not. The expression 'a universal moral right' may be used in a stronger sense or in a weaker sense. In the stronger sense it means a right of all men against all men; in the weaker sense it means simply a right of all men, but not necessarily against all men. In the weaker sense, all men may have a right which is, for each of them, a right against some men only. An example or two will make this clear. Every man has a moral right against every man not to be killed; i.e., every man has a duty to every man not to kill him. This is a universal right in the stronger sense. By contrast, every man has a right, when a child, to parental care, but this is not a right against every man; i.e., it is not the duty of every man to give to every child the care of a parent. Now the economic and social rights, and likewise the political right of participation in government, are universal rights in the weaker sense. When the Universal Declaration says that every man has the right to work, or the right to subsistence, it does not imply that the corresponding responsibility to provide any particular man with work or subsistence rests on every other man or every group of men; it implies that this responsibility rests on the members of his own State, and that the government of that State has a duty to carry out the responsibility on behalf of all its members. We do of course speak of a responsibility to help people who are in need in other parts of the world, but such help is an act of benevolence or charity, and not a matter of implementing a right. Similarly, the political right of participation in government applies only within one's own State. An Englishman has the right to participate in the government of Great Britain but not to participate in the government of France; and since there is no World State, it makes no sense to speak of a right to participate in the government of mankind as a whole.

There is therefore a genuine difference between the rights of liberty on the one hand and political, economic, and social rights on the other. It is well expressed by the French distinction between 'the rights of man' and 'the rights of the citizen'. One has the rights of liberty simply as a member of the human race, and they are rights which link every man with every other man. One has political, economic, and social rights as a member of a particular civil society, and these rights link each man with all the other members of his society.

While this distinction limits 'the rights of man' or 'human rights' to the rights of liberty, it does not justify any suggestion that the rights of the citizen, i.e., the political, economic, and social rights, should not be included in an international declaration. Although the Universal Declaration has led to the establishment of a regional international court, the European Court of Human Rights, and may well lead to further international institutions, nevertheless the main purpose of the Declaration is to encourage national governments to promote legislation and administrative measures for securing the rights of individuals within their own States. Legislation by governments of course encompasses the rights of men as citizens and not merely the rights which they have as human beings. Some people may say that the Universal Declaration taken by itself, without international machinery for implementation, can have no effect on the actions of national governments. I myself do not share this view. Despite the lack of realism in some of the annual reports made by governments, I think that the influence of the Declaration and of the reports, by the force of example, is not negligible. However, this is a practical question, on which the theorist had best hold his tongue. So far as the analysis of concepts is concerned, I have tried to show where there is not, and where there is, a difference of principle between two kinds of rights in the Universal Declaration.

SIX

BERNARD MAYO

What are Human Rights?

RECENT discussions[1] of this subject seem to reveal substantial agreement not only (of course) on the normative questions involved but also on the main questions of analysis. Disagreement and uncertainty enter into the more detailed points of analysis, and it has become clear to all that an enormous complexity in the key terms both of legal and of moral language must rule out any definitive set of answers.

Professor Raphael has not convinced me that there is anything startlingly new to be said about human rights, and I shall limit myself to expressing disagreement with him over certain basic conceptual points, finally offering an alternative interpretation of what he claims as a major distinction between two classes of human rights.

I

I shall assume that the traditional expressions 'Human Rights', 'Natural Rights', and 'Inalienable Rights' are for present purposes interchangeable. A brief defence of this assumption would be as follows. Human beings could have natural rights which were not human rights only if either (i) *all* men had rights in virtue of belonging to some wider 'natural' class — if, for instance, all living things had rights (biological rights) — or (ii) *some* men had rights in virtue of some 'natural' property or other which distinguished them from other men, such as skin colour or ancestry. In fact, however, all 'natural rights' theories, and all their 'human rights' successors, have assumed that neither (i) nor (ii) is the case. Human rights are the rights that a human being has in virtue of whatever characteristics he has that are both specifically and universally human. Being rational, and being capable of choice, are two such characteristics (or perhaps, after all, one) that are frequently mentioned. A more interesting set is the five 'salient characteristics of human nature' which Professor H. L. A. Hart lists (in another connexion) as the foundation of the 'minimum content of natural law'.[2] In so far as natural rights are what are guaranteed by natural law (a traditional assumption I shall not rely on), Hart's characteristics could be regarded as those in virtue of which human beings have human rights. It is interesting to note that Hart regards all the items in the list as 'simple truisms', whereas Stuart M. Brown, for example, thinks that 'scientific studies' have been required to prove that man's interests and capacities are in fact universal.[3]

These rights are 'natural' because, and in whatever sense, the characteristics are. Of course the connexion between having the characteristics and having the rights is not itself 'natural' — whatever that might mean. Nor is it 'artificial' or 'conventional' either. But, as I shall be affirming later, it is *we* who claim rights for men.

Finally, human rights are 'inalienable' just because a man cannot choose to divest himself of his human nature, nor, consequently, of anything which is entailed thereby, though he can certainly transfer rights which are not 'natural', such as ownership, by an 'artificial' act, such as giving.

II

Rights are said to be conferred, claimed, granted, exercised, invoked, revoked, waived, forfeited, vindicated, enjoyed, and possessed — to mention but a few verbs which take 'rights' as their objects. Most of these verbs will also take as objects most of a great variety of other terms: titles, privileges, authority, power; while a range of verbs, *entitle, authorize, empower*, testifies to the close involvement between verb and object, amounting quite often to an 'internal accusative'. Two suggestions are implied here. First, we should be on our guard against any tendency to assume that rights are the sort of entities whose existence can be asserted independently of a context of institutional activities of the sort indicated by the list of verbs. This would exclude one — but not, of course, the only — interpretation of the phrase 'Natural Rights'; but it would not exclude all non-positivistic views:

it would not exclude a view that human rights are founded in a transcendental order, provided that conferments, revocations, and so on, were activities that a transcendental being could engage in. The second suggestion operates in the reverse direction. Just because our discussion never could have been proposed under the name 'Human Entitlements', we ought to be asking what there is about rights, as distinct from titles, empowerings, and authorizations, that enables us to assert their existence *at some remove* from actual institutional contexts.

I shall speak of rights as arising primarily from *undertakings*; and in Sections IV and VI, I shall examine the possibility of asserting rights in general, and human rights in particular, which do not so arise.

III

My first main disagreement with Raphael is a serious one because, if I am not mistaken, one of his major distinctions is involved in it. First let me summarize the distinctions he wishes to draw:

(1) Rights of action/rights to act

(2) Rights of recipience

which subdivides into two:

(2a) Rights to liberty, rights to be *allowed* to act

(2b) Rights to opportunity, rights to be *given* something.

I accept the distinction between (2a) and (2b), and I shall enlarge on it later. It is a generalized form of the distinction between Hart's 'natural right' to 'freedom' and Brown's 'inalienable right' to 'protection of private interests by government institutions'.[4] It should be noted at once, though, that over a large range of cases the difference is more schematic than real. When Raphael says 'opportunity or more than opportunity' he betrays an uneasiness on this score; liberty shades imperceptibly into opportunity and opportunity into actual giving; and this indeterminacy is inevitable, for there are all possible combinations of effort-sharing in the attainment of what one has a right to, from the maximum effort on the part of the right-owner combined with the merest passivity of the person or institution against whom he has the right, to the merest passivity of the recipient combined with the maximum effort on the part of the giver. Despite this, however, it is very important to distinguish the two ends of the spectrum.

I do not accept, though, the distinction between (1) and (2), and accordingly I am also able to reject the awkward distinction between rights to *act* and rights to be *allowed* to act. The original distinction is, I think, based on a misunderstanding of the common diction 'You have no right to . . .'. A right to act, according to Raphael,[5] is simply that a person has a right to do X, if (and only if) X is not wrong. If X is wrong, he has no right to do X. Now it is true that we often say things like 'She had no right to . . .', 'You have no right to . . .', where we mean just that what she did, or what you are contemplating doing, is wrong. But what this does *not* mean is that there is a right to do X, which she lacked, or you lack, and which she or you would enjoy, if X were not wrong. The affirmative cases soon show this up. A cynical adulterer, asked whether he thought his seduction of another man's wife is wrong, might sincerely say 'It's not wrong'; but this would be very far indeed from saying 'I have a right to seduce her'! Where the discrepancy is not so glaring, it is, I suggest, for the following reason. We have the convenient locutions 'You ought not to have done/be doing/do X' to express adverse judgements about deeds done, doing, or contemplated; but we have no convenient locutions for the corresponding contradictories. We have circumlocutions like 'It was not wrong (or it was right) of you to do X', 'It is a right thing you are doing', 'It would be right if you were to do X', etc. Now since 'A has a right to do X' is in use (albeit a different use) it is not difficult to understand how it should come to be doing double duty; and how *its* contradictory 'A has no right to do X' should come to do double duty for the original 'A ought not to do X'.

I therefore deny that a person has a right of action, as distinct from having a right to be allowed to act, or a right of recipience to freedom from interference, as Raphael puts it. What appears to him to be the other sort of right (type (1)) is merely a matter of idiom: more perspicuously, if more pedantically, expressed as a right*ness*. The difference clearly emerges in the difference between his example and Carritt's: Carritt's example of an *act*, the right to which is equivalent to a duty on the part of others not to prevent it, was 'entering', which is, of course, without further specification, morally neutral; while Raphael's example is 'kicking a boy downstairs without provocation', which is, of course, without further specification, morally wrong.

I think Raphael goes even further astray when he claims that the two kinds of right are not merely distinct, but that the second is actually dependent on the first: 'it is only when . . . his proposed action is itself not wrong or unlawful . . . that he has the second right to freedom from interference' (p. 56). It follows from this not only that a man never has a right to freedom from interference in illegal conduct (which we may allow) but also that he never has a right to freedom from interference in *immoral* conduct either; and this is totally unacceptable. Even if we were to agree (as I, and I am sure Raphael, would not) that a person engaging in immoral conduct of whatever kind ought always to be interfered with, this substantive moral conclusion could not possibly follow from a conceptual analysis of what a right is. The only escape from this is to equivocate on the term 'interfere', holding that in moral contexts it is to be interpreted as 'disapprove' or something of that sort. But there is no hint in Raphael's paper that he is prepared to extend the sphere of rights and duties from actions to states of mind; and it is as well that there is not, for this would open up staggering new problems.

IV

I next want to examine the doctrine of the correlativity of rights and duties.

Duties have been traditionally divided into duties of perfect obligation, which do imply correlative rights, and duties of imperfect obligation, which do not. An example of the former would be my duty to keep a promise: the person to whom the promise was made has a right to my fulfilment of it. An example of the latter is my duty to perform acts of charity, or to devote myself to promoting disarmament; in neither case are there any specific persons who have rights against me. It has also been suggested that a similar distinction holds for rights: 'perfect' rights being those like, again, the right to the fulfilment of a promise, where a correlative duty lies on a specific person; and 'imperfect' rights, where no specific person has a duty to give me what I have a right to; and rights occurring in a typical list of 'human rights' might seem to be examples of the latter.

This second suggestion is a mistake. It is true that I have discharged my obligation to perform acts of charity (at least on a not too exacting standard of what this requires) when I have appropriately succoured an arbitrary set of individuals; indeed, if the set were conspicuously not arbitrary, my charitable motives would be suspected. But it is certainly not true that a man's right to be protected from starvation is vindicated, if it so happens that a random series of passers-by remedies his plight. Nor is his right to £1,000 a year, if he thinks he has such a right, vindicated by a run of luck on the football pools. It cannot be true, then, that no specific person or persons has a duty to vindicate the rights mentioned in a list of human rights. What is true is only that this person, or these persons, are not readily identifiable. Human rights, as I shall affirm more forcibly later on, are secured by political action, and are claimed of political authorities. What is unclear is not where the duties lie, but in what sense a State can be an agent. If it can, then it can also have duties; if not, the duties must lie on its agents, representatives, functionaries — whoever they are.

The doctrine of the correlativity of duties and rights is true only of the limited class of duties and rights generated by *undertakings* — including promises and contracts. It does not extend to all duties the discharge of which involves a specific person or persons, and this person does not always have a right against the person who has the duty. In particular, a person who is *concerned*, however directly and specifically, in the duty-discharging act never has a right to that act unless there is an undertaking, express or implied, made *to* that person. The hackneyed textbook example will serve here as well as any: I should regard it as my duty to try to save a drowning child, but neither the child, nor anyone else, ever has a right to my assistance in attempting to save his life. This sounds a hard saying, but I hasten to add that it is intended to be fully consistent with my being as conscientious as the next man about succouring those in distress. My point is just that, however extreme my devotion to duty, however deep my sensitivity to the charge of callousness if I were to stand idly by, etc., etc., it is just a misdescription of the situation to say that the drowning child has a right against me which he vindicates by having me attempt to rescue him. A glance at the list of verbs that go with 'rights', with which I began Section II, confirms that the word is out of place here; if it is used at all, and I do not deny that in the heat of the moment it might be, it is an extended use, just

F   R.P.T.

as the use I criticized in Section III was an extended use. The extension is a natural one, because many of the characteristic features of situations involving a moral duty are also features of situations involving rights, especially when the discharge of the duty concerns, or benefits, another person. But I see no need to assimilate the two by making 'rights' apply to both, as Hart, for instance, does when he speaks of the moral obligation to obey the rules of any system, including those of political society, as 'due to the co-operating members of the society' who therefore have a right to the submission of the others;[6] and general rights (to freedom) entail as correlatives 'obligations not to interfere to which everyone else is subject'. Everyone, then, has a right to the submission of everyone to the rules of all systems in which they are joint members, and everyone has obligations not to interfere with anyone. This proliferation of rights and duties, in the interest of maintaining the correlativity thesis, seems to me to emasculate both concepts.

But now a dilemma appears. Any duties which are correlative with *human rights* will be duties the discharge of which *concerns* all men; but it is not easy to see how they arise from undertakings *to* their beneficiaries. If they do not, then, on the view just stated, human rights — rights claimed on behalf of all men — are not rights at all. And I certainly do not accept this conclusion.

To solve this problem we must, I think, turn to consider an aspect of rights which Professor Raphael has strangely neglected.

V

Professor Raphael uses, but does not discuss, some of the vocabulary in which 'rights' is embedded. He speaks only once of rights being 'conferred'; only in two passages of rights being 'claimed'; and apart from the neutral idioms 'having a right' and 'there being a right', he cautiously relies on speaking of our *speaking* of rights; occasionally and more venturously, of rights being 'declared', 'enunciated', 'introduced', of occurring in, or being 'struck out of', a 'list'. I want to be much more daring; I want to select the elements in that rich vocabulary which show the concept of 'rights' operating, so to speak, on its home ground. I shall select the verb and noun pairs 'claim' and 'demand'. For a right to exist, in any but an extended, parasitic, or trivialized sense, is for a right to have been granted; for a right to have been granted, a right will have been claimed; and for a right to be claimed is simply for a claim to be made. In short, a right is just a claim: perhaps a special sort of claim, though I do not think that any drastic qualification is necessary. I propose the following definitions:

(A) A right is a claim.

(B) A human right is a claim, on behalf of all men, to corporate action (or perhaps inaction) on the part of whatever institution is in a position to satisfy the claim (normally, the institution(s) of which all men are necessarily members, i.e., States).

I proceed to annotate each of (A) and (B).

(A) An obvious first objection to (A) as it stands is that rights can exist without being claimed. A man can have a right which he never has claimed and never will. And when a right is claimed, so it will be said, the right is a substantive object of the claim and not a mere internal accusative. But consider my claiming an umbrella. Certainly the umbrella exists independently of my claiming it. But claiming an umbrella is not doing something to an umbrella: it is asserting my ownership of the article. And it is hard to see that my right (of ownership) exists quite independently of my claims to it. Could an umbrella be *mine* if I never claimed it as mine nor ever had the least tendency to do so? (We must, I think, supplement 'claiming' with 'being disposed to claim'.) The only class of rights which can plausibly be detached from claims seems to be rights (including ownership) which the possessor *does not know that he has*. Even this class is still further reduced by pointing out that a man may have rights which, if he does not claim them, or is not disposed to claim them, for himself, are claimed *on his behalf* by someone else. I have not said that the owner of a right is necessarily the claimant of the right; and this class of rights claimed on behalf of others is, according to (B), the class to which human rights belong.

If there are any rights which can be conferred on a man without his knowledge, and without any claim either by him or on his behalf, they could still be related to claims: they could be regarded as the granting in advance of claims not yet made, or as the recognition of valid grounds for possible claims. But I prefer to treat this class as marginal. Even if the general concept of 'rights' could be understood by reference to it (which I strongly doubt), the special concept of 'human rights' certainly could not.

Next after the objection that not all rights are claims, is the objection that not all claims are rights. For although (A) itself does not imply that all claims are rights, calling it a definition does; and this is questionable. But what sort of *differentiae* are called for? Qualifications which might be attached to 'claim' in (A) will, I think, turn out to be otiose.

(*a*) A right is a *justified*, or at least a *justifiable*, claim: we speak of claiming something *as of right*, which suggests that only some claims are justified or justifiable. But either qualification is otiose. A *demand* can be (totally) unjustified and unjustifiable, like the bank-robber's demand to hand over the cash. But can a *claim* be (totally) unjustified and unjustifiable? I hardly think so. Even a medieval seigneur, barbarous as his claims may have been by present-day standards, had presumably some token justification at hand. The only sense in which a claim can be unjustified is the sense in which, say, a claim for an extra £5 a week for postmen might be unjustified. But it would not be a claim if the postmen, at least, thought it unjustified. 'I claim X, but there is no reason at all why you should give me X' is self-contradictory; even if 'He claims X, but there is no reason at all why you should give him X' is not.

(*b*) A right is a claim *for something that is in one's interest*. We do not often claim things that we do not want; perhaps we sometimes do. But we also, perhaps, have rights to things we do not want.

(*c*) A right is a claim *for something that is due in virtue of an undertaking*. Many claims (Hart's 'special rights') are claims to the fulfilment of a promise, contract, or similar undertaking; and I have said that all rights *which are correlative with duties* are of this kind. But are all claims tied to undertakings? I think that, if we are allowed to extend 'undertakings' to include participation in organizational systems, this will be true. A claim for higher wages on behalf of a class of workers, for instance, is admittedly not a claim to the fulfilment, by the management, of a promise to give them just that increase in pay; but in calling it a *claim*, rather than a *demand*, they are invoking the general undertakings, whether express or implied, which the conditions of employment carry.

(B) First, a *human right*, as distinct from a right, is a claim *on behalf of all men*. 'On behalf of' is a tricky expression: it cannot be said to be a claim *by* all men, for very few people actually make the claim; nor can it be called a claim to certain acts *for* (the benefit of) all men, since this would be consistent with most men having no say in the matter of what they are to get. Without entering on the very difficult topic of how men can be 'represented' by other men, we can, perhaps, suggest that claims 'on behalf of' other men are claims which those others, or at least a majority of them, *would* themselves make, or endorse, if they were in a position to make and understand them.

Next, a human right is a claim to *action* (or inaction) *by a State government*. The reasons for this qualification are historical rather than conceptual. (Here again I shall disagree with Raphael.) To begin with, many claims that could be made on behalf of all men do not figure in a list of human rights. Claims that could be made on behalf of all men will be claims to the fulfilment of any duty that any man owes to every man. These will certainly include the duty that a man has to every man not to kill him — discounting doubts that I have about this class of 'duties', and taking Raphael's example, which presumably carries the usual exception clause, and which Raphael speaks of as the right of every man not to be killed. They will also, as surely, include the duty which a man has to every man to tell him the truth when asked for information — again with the usual exceptions — which could with as much propriety be spoken of as the right of every man to be told the truth. But do these 'rights' figure in lists of human rights? Of course not; no Universal Declaration is concerned with protecting my life against homicidal persons; nor could such a Declaration be intended to promote truth-telling in general.[7] What a Declaration mentioning these topics *is* concerned with is, rather, to protect my life, and my ability to seek the truth, against the State itself: to claim for me freedom from arbitrary execution, or educational opportunities undistorted by propaganda.

I wish, then, to invert Raphael's order of conceptual priority among so-called 'human rights'. What he begins by calling a 'real and important difference among human rights' ends with the stultifying conclusion that one of the classes thus distinguished — and the very class of rights with which governments are mostly concerned — are not properly described as human rights at all. For this second class of rights — the Political, Economic, and Social Rights, distinguished as rights to be *given*, rather than *allowed*, something — are not human rights, according to Raphael. His reason is that they link a man only with other members of his society, while human rights properly so called link every man with every other man. If these 'rights of the citizen' do figure in a list of human rights, this calls for a special explanation: it is because the 'main' purpose of such a list is to 'encourage national governments to promote legislation and administrative measures' of a certain sort.

I invert this order of priority by making 'the rights of the citizen' the prime ingredient in a typical list of human rights. What Raphael rightly calls the main purpose of the Declaration is not a conceptual deviation. Human rights are *human* because they are claimed on behalf of all men; but it is necessary to ask, *of whom* are they claimed? Not, despite Raphael, of all men; rather, in my view, they are claims of, on, or against certain agents: namely (in the historical contexts in question) the national governments whose representatives are concerned in the issue, and reception, of the Declarations. I want to emphasize, then, Miss Margaret Macdonald's somewhat understated point, that the right to be told the truth, or to gratitude for favours given, 'are not inscribed on banners carried by aggrieved demonstrators'; and to endorse Professor Hart's remark: 'Men speak of their moral rights mainly when advocating their incorporation in a legal system'.

Another reason for challenging Raphael's conclusion is this. Analysis of concepts, with which he professes to have been concerned, cannot wait on the facts of political history. Now it is a fact of political history that there is no world government; but this cannot possibly make the difference between the right of participation in government being, or not being, a human right. Indeed, the United Nations Declaration virtually announces a right to world government.

VI

It remains to solve the problem I set myself by insisting that rights imply undertakings. In speaking of rights in general (under (A)), I spoke of claims which invoke an undertaking which was not an undertaking to give precisely and specifically what is the content of the claim, but something more general. In the case of claims made on behalf of all men, however, it may well seem that any undertaking we might look for to support such a claim must be vanishingly thin.

There are two answers to this. First, it is a commonplace of political theory that the agents of government have certain duties to perform on behalf of the citizens; the precise nature and foundation of these duties is notoriously obscure, but the constant tendency to look for some kind of *contractual* relation shows, I think, that we do assume the existence of some undertaking which is not vanishingly thin. For any group of people co-operating in a joint enterprise by means of rules there will be this class of rights at least: the members have a right to the discharge of duties by officers and functionaries. In so far as the State, then, 'undertakes' to protect the lives and property of its citizens, it thereby recognizes their rights.

But this does not take us very far towards human rights. For the very point of a Declaration is, as Raphael and I agree, to promote government recognition of rights which it has not, as yet, undertaken to recognize. A government which has not yet disbanded its secret police, or provided free education for all, or instituted welfare services for the sick or elderly, will consider a Declaration of Human Rights, mentioning such things, as inviting it to undertake new obligations for its citizens. Or is it, rather, being invited to acknowledge obligations which it already has? It matters little, for present purposes, what we are to say here. What does matter is that a government, and only a government, *can* undertake to provide, for its citizens, what is claimed on behalf of all men.

Once we leave the solid ground of specific promises and contracts, where the concept of a right is most clearly and unambiguously displayed, we have a continuous series of cases: promises which are not absolutely specific; vague promises; positions of responsibility; obligation-incurring situations; and in all of these there is room for debate as to just what a person ought to do, or what another person ought to receive. In the end, of course, we arrive at a moral judgement. But the concept of 'rights' does not evaporate at some point in this range of decreasing specificity. All I feel confident of saying at present is that there are points beyond which it has evaporated, as in my example of saving the drowning child (an 'obligation-incurring situation'); at the point of government ('positions of responsibility') it has not. *Why* it has not, in this case, I have just been trying to suggest.

SEVEN

PETER SCHNEIDER

Social Rights and the Concept of Human Rights

E VEN in the twentieth century political thought and activity are
determined largely by the classical doctrine of the rights of man.
According to this doctrine each individual, by virtue of belonging to
the *gens humana*, has inalienable rights. Indeed, if one does not let
oneself be misled by day-to-day events, it becomes apparent that the
great political controversy between Liberal Democracy and Com-
munism is pursued under the rubric of human rights. It is pursued
moreover in such a way that both sides to the quarrel consider themselves as the appointed guardians of these rights, and mutually reproach
each other with their violation. If, for some, the system of economic
exploitation hiding, according to them, behind the façade of Liberal
Democracy is in total contradiction to human rights, for others the
so-called liberation of the proletariat and the development towards true
humanity in the Communist sense are really a pretext leading to slavery
and to the establishment of the totalitarian power of party and State,
to which the rights of the individual are exposed without protection.
Finally one also cannot deny that the third great political movement
which is being realized in our time, the emancipation of the colonial
peoples, is being carried out under the banner of the doctrine of human
rights, that national self-determination and human rights are seen as
linked together.

In these circumstances the question of the content of the classical
doctrine on the one hand, and of the present-day doctrine on the other,
is particularly pressing. Perhaps the expression, 'the rights of man',
should mean for us something quite different from what it meant in the
eighteenth century. Or rather, would it not be worth interpreting
present tendencies in the light of their historical origin, unless we want

to risk getting lost in the primeval forest of political phrases and slogans?

I

The *classical* doctrine of the rights of man, which was developed in the Anglo-Saxon countries, in France, and in Germany, cannot be interpreted either exclusively as an unconditional negation of the State, or exclusively as an unconditional affirmation of the State. The 'cases' of unconditional negation and affirmation of the State must, however, be considered as extreme positions in relation to the classical doctrine. (1) According to the anarchist point of view, the State constitutes *the* danger which threatens the spread of liberty and equality. (2) According to the Jacobin point of view, the State appears as the creator of liberty and equality, because it has the monopoly of *education* and of *force*.

It follows from this that one also cannot identify the classical doctrine of the rights of man with a completely liberal doctrine, according to which the only things that matter are the emancipation of the middle classes and a reduction in the power of the State. Both in the American Constitution and in the French Declaration of 1789, there appears quite clearly a desire to compromise between the freedom *to live without interference* from the State and the freedom *to participate* in its affairs, and also between freedom and security. As for the German doctrine, one can cite Kant's theory of the constitutional State, which, starting from the axiom of liberty and equality, demands that the State should possess the right of constraint, regulated by laws, and that there should be a separation of powers.

It would be just as false to interpret the classical doctrine of the rights of man as an *unlimited individualism*. Indeed, one must not forget that the classical doctrine of the rights of man is determined by the conviction that, independently of his social or national affiliations, independently of his belonging to the 'class' of rich or poor, the individual enjoys autonomy because he is or ought to be a member of the *gens humana* and a rational being. But, in addition, it must be noted that even Rousseau has accepted Montesquieu's theory of 'the general in the particular'.

So it is not surprising that, in the classical doctrine of the rights of man, the freedom of the individual is in no case identical with *freedom from all obligation.* Hobbes's theory about the 'natural' unlimited liberty of the individual, according to which liberty and 'the freedom to devour and be devoured' are one and the same thing, entails the absolutist theory of the State, which is clearly opposed to the classical doctrine of the rights of man. The classical theory of natural law, which is connected with the classical doctrine of the rights of man, presents natural law as a system of individual rights *and obligations* (cf. Raphael's essay). In the realm of German culture, one can again refer to Kant's theory, according to which natural law, like positive law, ought to bring about the co-ordination of those who possess liberty at the same time. According to this theory, too, everyone has the *duty* to respect the liberty of others, as well as the *right* to demand respect for his own liberty in conformity with the universal law and to obtain it by compulsion.

Moreover, the classical theory of natural law does not exclude the duty of mutual aid. According to Kant, the individual ought not only to respect the aspiration of others to 'happiness', but even *to encourage* it. In addition to the duty of mutual aid, which, in the framework of the family and the domestic community, for example, appears not only as a moral but also as a legal obligation, mention must be made here of the legal duty of the State *to help the poor* — a duty which is linked with the classical doctrine of the rights of man. In this connexion it must be remembered that, particularly according to the Jacobin conception, it is the duty of the State to create an *economic equality.* Finally it is relevant to point out that compulsory public education — this obligatory 'culture' — cannot be dissociated from the classical doctrine of the rights of man.

There is no doubt that the classical doctrine of the rights of man is concerned in the first instance with the relationship between *individuals* and the *State.* Nevertheless, two points must not be overlooked: first, that, as we have shown, classical natural law stems from *legal relationships* between individuals, which are guaranteed by the State. Secondly, that the family is generally envisaged as a *natural community,* and that, on the other hand, according to the *principle of self-determination* — taken along with that of the separation of powers — importance is given to social institutions which are not State-controlled.

II

All these considerations allow one to conclude that although the classical doctrine of the rights of man can be connected ideologically with extreme positions, it nevertheless found expression both in the American Constitution and in the French Declaration of 1789. In these, freedom from governmental interference and freedom to participate in government (*die Freiheit vom Staat und die Freiheit zum Staat*) complemented each other. We can also conclude that in their theoretical context there was no hint of domination by a radical individualism, blind to social obligations and social structures not organized by the State. And there was just as little domination by a theory of liberty which confused liberty with doing as one pleased. Starting off from this finding, we can determine more exactly the connexion between the classical and the modern doctrines of human rights.

This connexion is not to be interpreted in the sense of an *antinomy*, but in the sense of a *gradual* differentiation. Even if one can notice a clear movement away from economic liberalism and towards a Welfare State providing social services — the evolution of the judgements of the American Supreme Court in matters of social and labour legislation provides an impressive demonstration of this — one ought not to ignore the fact that already a Georg Jellinek, in his general theory of the State, did not look on the intensifying of the drive towards social security as in any way a weakening, but rather as a strengthening, of individual freedoms. There was accordingly a continuous and gradual evolution towards the idea of social solidarity, the idea that man is to be understood not as an isolated individual but as a 'person living in a community', that humanity means sympathy with one's fellow-men, that consideration must be given to Fraternity as well as to Liberty and Equality. Moreover the practical significance of such ideas became greater and greater, and this evolution would certainly not be intelligible but for violent changes and advances in radical movements.

From the idea of social solidarity there follows a much greater openmindedness, both in theory and in practice, in dealing with those situations in which even an adult individual is referred to the help of the community; it is better understood that it is not enough to proclaim general freedoms, that for many reasons it is essential first to create the prerequisites for the exercise of freedom. So there grew up a far-reaching network of social institutions, social insurances, such as old-age and dependants' pensions, initial help of all kinds, compensation funds, and provident schemes. All these are financed partly by the State and partly by private organizations. Legislative measures directed towards the equalization of material burdens belong to the same category. Finally all these measures and institutions are to be understood from the standpoint of a modern conception of human rights. For this conception, it is not enough to postulate, for instance, free expression of opinion as such; it is important not to interfere with the process of the formation of public opinion and to keep it free from monopolization.

On the other hand, there arises from this basic point of view an enhanced awareness of the significance of non-State social institutions, of the hazards and risks to individuals which they entail. For instance, the family is understood and encouraged not only as a necessary, natural community, but as that social structure in which the individual as a community-orientated person receives the basis of his education and the protection which no large organization is in a position to give him. The idea of self-government is given a considerable significance also under varying conditions, on the one hand in the form of local administrative autonomy, on the other in the form of economic and social administrative autonomy, which, so far as the shaping of conditions of work is concerned, is taken care of by trade unions and employers' associations. The fact that more attention is paid to political parties and that they are increasingly an object of scientific analysis and legislative efforts is also comprehensible from this basic point of view.

Thus there is connected with the doctrine of human rights a doctrine of social *pluralism*, and the dangers of this must be recognized. First, one must point out the danger that theory and practice draw the individual more and more into a plurality of social structures which are not connected with the State but which, by their power and bureaucratic ways, often resemble State institutions; consequently the individual can only acquire recognition in the category of outsiders, of the maladjusted. On the other hand there is the danger that individual selfishness will be replaced by a group selfishness which has nothing at all to do with the idea of fraternity, of the brotherhood of man. This danger — it can be indicated as the opposite danger to totalitarianism — corresponds to the danger of anarchy, which has in the past threatened the classical doctrine of the rights of man.

In harmony with this attitude, the point of view of social security and justice is stressed in the important declarations of human rights in our day, side by side with the so-called liberal rights. Already in the Atlantic Charter of 14 August 1941 the aim was clearly declared of guaranteeing improved working conditions, economic equality, and social security for all, by means of the closest economic co-operation between nations.

In the Preamble to the United Nations Charter, there is mentioned the belief in fundamental human rights, in the dignity and value of the human person, as well as in social progress and a higher standard of living with greater freedom. In the Universal Declaration of Human Rights of 10 December 1948 along with liberal and political rights and the claim to legal protection, there is mentioned, amongst other things, the right to social security, to the economic, social, and cultural means indispensable for free development, the right to work, to appropriate payment and measures of social protection, to recreation and leisure, to security in case of illness, disablement, old age, and the right to education, beginning with free elementary education. In the Convention of 4 November 1950, on the Protection of Human Rights and Fundamental Freedoms, reference is made to the so-called Universal Declaration and to the rights contained therein, including social rights. In the catalogue of rights guaranteed by the Convention, however, there are no guarantees corresponding to the social rights of the Universal Declaration. In the Declaration of New Delhi, which was formulated in New Delhi by the International Commission of Jurists, the first section says: 'It is the duty of the Legislature in a free society under the rule of law to create and maintain conditions which safeguard the dignity of man as an individual. That dignity requires not only the recognition of his political and civil rights, but also the creation of social, economic, educational, and cultural conditions which are essential for the full development of the personality.' Unlike the Universal Declaration of Human Rights, and in agreement with the European Convention, the New Delhi Declaration makes no attempt to draw up a list of the social rights of individuals and the corresponding social duties of States.

III

Let us discuss the difficulties and the problems inherent in the realization of the postulate of 'fraternity' and social rights by the example of the Bonn Basic Law.

The Basic Law is directed towards the central value of *human dignity*. According to Article 1, § 1, the dignity of man is regarded as *inviolable*, and it is a duty of all State power *to respect* and *to defend* human dignity. The basis and the limit of the power of the State are thus determined by human dignity.

First of all, human dignity is significant as the foundation of human rights. Because they constitute the basis and limit of State power, the German people recognizes inviolable and inalienable human rights 'as the foundation of every human community, of peace and justice in the world' (Basic Law, Article 1, § 2).

From the theoretical point of view, it is worth noting that the authors of the Basic Law try to make it clear that the basic structure, not only of order within the State, but also of order between States, of international order, derives from the idea of human dignity and human rights. Moreover the same attempt can be seen in the European Convention on Human Rights, in which reference is made to the basic freedoms 'which constitute the foundations of justice and peace in the world'. One may think little of the practical value of such formulae: nevertheless they give expression to the effort to break down the rigid barriers between national and international law, and to conceive of legal order as a whole, as an indivisible system of values.

On the other hand, there is eminent practical value in Article 1, § 3, of the Basic Law: 'The following basic rights are obligatory for legislation, administration, and judicial decision, as directly valid law.' This formula opposes the opinion that basic rights only represent a programme, which it is the task of the legislator to put into effect. On the other hand, it is not opposed to the opinion that the list of basic rights is to be thought of as an *open* list, that not only are the rights mentioned in it guaranteed by the Basic Law, but rather that all individual rights which can be derived from the principle of human dignity and which are capable of realization one day, are so guaranteed.

If one scrutinizes the whole list of basic rights, it is clear that it enumerates essentially the so-called classical rights of liberty, the right to free development of the personality, the principle of equality, freedom of faith and creed, freedom of speech, the right to private property, etc. There is hardly any mention, however, of basic social rights in the sense of claims to State provision. On the other hand there are in this list prescriptions for the protection of the family (that is to say, of a non-State social structure), prescriptions which can hardly be put into the framework of individual rights. Moreover, amongst these prescriptions is one covering the mother's claim to the protection and care of the community, a social right from two points of view: social in so far as it points to social action, and social in so far as it cannot be described as a right which belongs to the individual as an individual, but as one which is derived from a *social relationship* and *function*. But more of that in another context.

In the catalogue of basic rights listed in the Basic Law there is, for example, no mention of a right to a minimum economic subsistence. Consequently the question arises whether such a right can be directly derived from the principle of human dignity. The question is controversial. Nevertheless it is indisputable that Article 1, § 1, together with the *principle of the social State*, which is firmly established in Article 20 of the Basic Law, implies that this right is to be described as fundamental. It is further indisputable that where the legislator has imposed on the State obligations for social action, the individual has at his disposal rights for which he can obtain satisfaction in a court of law.

It follows that, according to the view of the authors of the Basic Law, it is, in the first place, *the business of the legislator* to put into effect the principle of the social State, to impose on the State obligations for social action and to grant corresponding individual rights. This attitude of the authors of the Basic Law corresponds to the fact that where declarations of human rights are directed towards practical implementation, as the European Convention or the New Delhi Declaration are directed towards the task of satisfying social claims, this task is either marginally indicated or considered as a duty of the legislator. It is also significant that the almost euphoric joy of the authors of the Universal

Declaration of Human Rights in specifying social rights has noticeably abated in the light of the efforts to draw up a universal convention on human rights. The reason for this is that it is easier *to forbid* State measures, in the form of subjective, terse rights, with intelligible consequences, than *to decree* them. Two examples: freedom of speech on the one hand, the right to work on the other. It is relatively easy to procure observance for a prohibition addressed to the State against interference with freedom of speech. On the other hand it would be enormously complicated to give effect to a right to work. Apart from the fact that such a right would only too easily come into conflict with the freedom to choose one's own profession, it cannot be given effect without the erection of a whole apparatus of authorities provided with far-reaching powers. On the other hand, of course, such structural objections must not be given too much weight. One must not overlook the fact that a group of publicly-recognized, subjective rights, which, as it happens, the European Convention and the Declaration of New Delhi have specially stressed, are linked, of logical necessity, with measures to be taken by the State. It is a question of the so-called *claims for the safeguarding of rights*. The right to the judge prescribed by statute implies, for example, a differentiated judicial organization. On the other hand one must not overlook the fact that giving effect to freedom of speech, for instance in the domain of television and radio, requires legislation in order to eliminate risks to the formation of opinion coming from public as well as from private quarters.

Nevertheless the whole body of opposing structures justifies the formula: *prohibitions against interference by the State can be better expressed in the form of subjective rights than as commands to intervene.*

An exception is formed by claims for the safeguarding of rights, which are guaranteed in the tradition of the constitutional State, claims such as the right to a minimum subsistence, which necessarily stems from the principle of human dignity and that of the social State. A further exception can be recognized in the *right to education*, which corresponds to *compulsory schooling*. At times it is presented as the right to share in the school arrangements which provide for elementary education. But then again it is presented as the right to share in them without being subjected to undue material burdens. Here it can be a question of the claim to the means of elementary education without charge, to grants in order to obtain teaching materials; finally it can be a question also of the right to the provision of educational establishments for children in remote districts, or at least to the provision of the necessary transport so that they can travel to existing schools. It goes without saying, that in this context, too, the realization of the right (or rights) depends on numerous legislative measures and administrative arrangements, and that a wide differentiation of claims is impossible. Yet it must be accepted that the principles set forth in the area of application of the Basic Law are presented in the form of subjective rights guaranteed by the constitution.

But besides — let us repeat — it appears to be simply the task of the legislator, resulting from the tenets of the social State and the principle of human dignity, to make arrangements to create social *equality* between different sections of the population, and social security, and to supplement formal equality by material equality.

The Basic Law assumes man to be a *social* person and not an isolated individual. This follows from the dignity of man and the principle of the social State. From this point of view one can understand the prescriptions which recognize the rights of *non-State social structures* or demand their protection. First of all, attention must again be drawn to the regulations for the protection of *marriage and the family*. These regulations are not, indeed, in opposition to those which guarantee the freedoms of the individual. The principle of monogamy is intimately linked with the principle of equal rights of husband and wife. The right of parents to educate their children clashes with totalitarian ideas which consider young people as belonging to the State, and is based on the hypothesis that the education of social persons is most easily assured in the family group, as being the group in which as a rule the personality comes completely to fruition. Finally, the prescriptions for the protection of the family are also inspired by the thought that relative security in the family group will reduce the risk that individuals will be exposed to totalitarian tendencies. The *'fédéralisme domestique'*, which was attacked by Robespierre, is accordingly at the service of the right to individual autonomy. In so far as one can derive subjective rights from the regulations of Article 6 of the Basic Law, it is not a question of rights which were originally individual, but of those which come from belonging to a group, of social rights in the sense of group rights.

Similar considerations apply in the realm of the right to self-government. The corporate bodies set up by Public Law, which are provided with rights of self-government and consequently with a certain independence from the State, are on the one hand useful for the fulfilment of necessary communal tasks and on the other hand serve the principle of *vertical division of powers*. If the principle of community self-government serves political freedom primarily, that of university self-government serves the freedom of teaching and research. Political freedom is again served by the granting of privileges to political parties as compared with other associations, according to Article 21 of the Basic Law. To be sure, legal practice and theory show that it is not altogether simple to understand adequately the position of political parties. The view that they are to be ranked with State-controlled bodies is untenable. It is more a question of non-State social structures to which has been delegated the public duty of facilitating the action of the politically active citizen, and which, as far as this duty is concerned, are entitled to specific, constitutionally guaranteed, social rights (in the sense of group rights). Their existence and effectiveness are nevertheless always dependent on the initiative and agreement of individual citizens.

Through group rights the Basic Law also gives an assured position to workers' and employers' organizations. It protects the so-called right of association by declaring null and void agreements which limit this right (Article 9, § 3). Further, it also gives a legal basis for the view that these organizations perform a public duty in protecting and improving conditions of work and industry. From this, it is also intelligible that the legislator delegates to the so-called social partners a certain legal power in matters of wage-regulation.

IV

Finally one must ask what is the connexion between the different categories of rights which have been discussed by means of these few examples.

Both the classical rights of the individual which protect him from interventions and encroachments by the power of the State, and also the political rights which assure to the individual a share in that power, derive from the principle of human dignity. They guarantee to the individual the possibility of self-determination economically, culturally, and politically. The same is true also of those social rights which oblige the State to do things for individuals, such as the right to a minimum subsistence, by means of which an existence fit for human beings is assured to every individual, and such as the right that corresponds to compulsory education, which is one of the foundations of self-determination. *No hierarchy of values*, as between these rights, is laid down. They are of equal rank. One would also not be justified in acknowledging a lesser rank for the specific group rights. Surely they too are finally directed towards an image of man as a social being.

Amongst these rights the relationship of *interdependence*, of *reciprocal conditioning*, is very important. They serve to develop the principle of human dignity. Political rights demand the so-called defence rights, and *vice versa*. Without elementary guarantees in economic matters, the other rights lose their meaning. Without an entitlement to elementary education, there can be no question of self-determination. Without freedom of association, the economic freedom of the worker is a mere formality. The right of parents to have their children educated assures the development of self-reliant and socially-minded persons.

Nevertheless the structural differences between the different categories of rights must not be ignored. It is no accident that social rights, in the form of entitlements to benefit and of group rights, are often described as creating the *conditions* under which the individual can achieve self-determination. Where these conditions are fulfilled, they cease to be urgently significant. This is particularly so in respect of *claims* to assistance from the State. The supposition that these conditions are not fulfilled is by no means valid everywhere. Rather the opposite is true, that the adult man who is adapted to his milieu and surroundings is capable of action on the basis of those rights which assure him freedom from State interference, as well as in the realm of political rights. This explains the rule, which is firmly established in administrative and constitutional procedure, that the individual must prove he has a claim to State provision, for example, while conversely, in the case of the limitation of economic freedoms, for example, it is the State which must provide the proof that there is a case for intervention, that without intervention there would be a serious danger for an important communal good. From this point of view, one can talk of a primacy of the so-called defence rights and political rights, as opposed to entitlement rights, which take on a subsidiary significance. If one were to reverse this relationship, which concerns not the value-rating of the rights in question but the mode of their realization, man would, unawares, be changed from a responsible subject into an object of State care and provision.

The situation is similar for the relationship between classical rights of liberty and political rights on the one hand, and group rights on the other. From the view that the individual cannot be conceived of without multiple group connexions, it does not follow that these groups are of primary importance. Even although the economic freedom of the individual worker cannot develop significantly without freedom of association, and without associations, the trade union does not replace the individual as the subject of economic freedom. In the same way, the individual is not replaced by the political party as the bearer of political rights because, without political parties, the active rights of citizens cannot be developed. Even if, from the recognition of the fact that man is a social being, one can derive a special category of group rights, these cannot be substituted for the primary individual rights, but take their place beside them. For this reason too it would be impossible, without suppressing the freedom of decision of individuals, to enforce compulsory membership of a party or a trade union.

The rights which allow to the individual freedom from governmental interference and freedom to participate in government (*Freiheit vom Staat und Freiheit zum Staat*) have primary importance in this sense, as against social rights in their double significance, although they are based on the same conception of values. Even if the rights which guarantee freedom from governmental interference are usually attributed to man as a member of the *gens humana*, and those which assure freedom of participation are attributed to man as a member of the State, there is nevertheless no difference in category between the rights of man and the rights of the citizen. A doctrine of human rights which originates in the conception of the fundamental value of human dignity must comprehend as a unity the rights of man, the rights of the citizen, and social rights, in all their interdependence and in all their differences.

The answer to totalitarian conceptions, which also appeal to the doctrine of human rights, can only be effective on the basis of a differentiating theory of man and code of law, which recognize unity in diversity, and look on man as a social being.

(Translated by Sylvia Raphael)

EIGHT

MAURICE CRANSTON

Human Rights:
A Reply to Professor Raphael

PROFESSOR RAPHAEL'S paper (V in this volume) is, I think, an important contribution to our understanding of the problem of human rights. His distinction between 'rights of recipience' and 'rights of action' is a very useful one, and I agree with him both when he says that Hobbes's idea of natural rights (as rights of action) is 'an aberration from the tradition that led to the concept of human rights' and when he says that 'human rights are rights of recipience, not rights of action'. But I cannot agree with Professor Raphael when he seeks, with the aid of this distinction, to provide a fresh justification for the now fashionable notion of universal economic and social rights. Indeed it seems to me that Professor Raphael slips altogether too easily from the acceptable suggestion that human rights are rights of recipience, rights to *receive* something, to the subtly different and bolder suggestion that such rights are rights to be *given* something, and thus to the conclusion that human rights can be seen as having a place in the economic or material realm, where 'giving' is understood as the transmission of objects from the hands of some to the hands of others.

My own view is quite otherwise. While I agree that human rights are rights to recipience, I would point out that what is received in this case is not something literally given; the giving is only metaphorical; what is rendered or bestowed is *respect*. And although respect is received and enjoyed, although respect can even, according to Dr. Johnson, be procured ('Fine clothes', he said, 'supply the want of other means of procuring respect'), respect is plainly not a thing that passes like a parcel from one man to another; respect is a characteristic of a man's behaviour or attitude towards another, namely the element of regard, consideration, or, if not necessarily of esteem, at least of non-interference. Professor Raphael, in another apt phrase, speaks of the traditional civil and political rights of man as 'rights of liberty'; and this helps us to see why the enjoyment of such rights turns on respect. Such rights are not given us by anybody; we have them already; the only thing needful is that they be acknowledged, recognized, respected.

Much has been made of the difference between rights and duties, and I think it an important one. But Tom Paine was surely correct when he said that there could be no rights without duties. To speak of a universal right is to speak of a universal duty; to say that all men have a right to life is to impose on all men the duty of respecting human life, to put all men under the same prohibition against attacking, injuring, or endangering the life of any other human being. Indeed, if this universal duty were not imposed, what sense could be made of the concept of universal human rights?

The so-called economic and social rights, in so far as they are intelligible at all, impose no such universal duty. They are rights to be given things, things such as a decent income, schools, and social services. But who is called upon to do the giving? Whose duty is it? When the authors of the United Nations Declaration of Human Rights assert that 'everyone has the right to social security', are they saying that everyone ought to subscribe to some form of world-wide social security system from which each in turn may benefit in case of need? If something of this kind is meant, why do the draft United Nations covenants, which are supposed to implement the Universal Declaration, make no provision for instituting such a system? And if no such system exists, where is the obligation, and where the right? To impose on men a 'duty' which they cannot possibly perform is as absurd in its way, though perhaps not as cruel, as bestowing on them a 'right' which they cannot possibly enjoy.

Professor Raphael, of course, says nothing so foolish. But I shall suggest that he is able to defend the idea of economic and social rights only at the expense of stripping them of their essential meaning. Professor Raphael writes: 'The expression "a universal moral right" may be used in a stronger sense or in a weaker sense. In the stronger sense it means a right of all men against all men; in the weaker sense it means simply a right of all men, but not necessarily against all men. In the weaker sense, all men may have a right which is, for each of them, a right against some men only.' One example of this 'weaker universal right' is the right men have against the government of their State; and it is into this category that Professor Raphael tries to fit some, though not quite all, of the economic and social rights named in the United Nations Declaration. Now this example, and what Professor Raphael says about it, serves, I am afraid, only to show that his so-called 'weaker universal right' is not a universal right at all; for in addition to being a right *against* some men only, it is a right which is *enjoyed* by some men only. Outside the economic and social rights that we are entitled to expect the government of our own State to confer, Professor Raphael goes on to say, 'We do of course speak of a responsibility to help people who are in need in other parts of the world, but such help is an act of benevolence or charity, and not a matter of implementing a right'. The outsider has no right. Thus the only economic and social rights that Professor Raphael is able to vindicate are *local* rights; the weakness of his 'weaker' universal economic and social rights is a radical weakness, a weakness unto death, for they have lost what is essential to the whole idea of the rights of man, and that is universality.

Professor Raphael notices an important distinction between the rights of man, *les droits de l'homme*, and the rights of the citizen, *les droits du citoyen*. But he does not seem to make the fullest use of this distinction, or to reflect on what follows from the decision to regard economic and social rights as part of the *droits du citoyen*, rather than as part of the *droits de l'homme*. For I should expect a theorist who noted this distinction to be closer to my view of the question than to that of the champions of universal economic and social rights.

Professor Raphael tries to correct me, as Professor Carl Friedrich has tried to correct me, for saying that 'economic and social rights were unknown to . . . the theorists of the eighteenth century', and he quotes claims made at that time by Babeuf and others. But I see no reason to withdraw my remark. The social and economic rights which were claimed by Babeuf and the others were not thought of as part of the universal rights of man; they were thought of as part of the distinctive rights of Frenchmen; as among *les droits du citoyen*, not among *les droits de l'homme*. And what makes this distinction all the more significant is that the justification Babeuf offered to support the case for the economic and social rights of Frenchmen was quite different from his justification of the civil and political rights of man.

Babeuf's argument for believing in the *droits de l'homme* was an ordinary conventional natural rights argument. His case for social and economic rights was a novel one. He adopted Locke's suggestion that a right to property must ultimately derive from the right to the product of one's own labour; but, rejecting the sophisticated pro-bourgeois form into which Locke himself developed this theory, Babeuf argued that the French labouring classes were the true makers of the wealth of France and therefore that those workers had each a right to possess each a fair share of that wealth. The basis of this 'social and economic right' is thus *desert*; the French labouring classes, on this argument, had by their labour *earned* their moral entitlement to be given something, or, rather, to be given something back. Moreover, there was no doubt in Babeuf's mind as to who should do the giving back — the French nobility and bourgeoisie, who had exploited the workers, and owed them this debt.

Professor Raphael quotes Tom Paine against me; but here again I suggest that Tom Paine is saying of England something very like what Babeuf is saying of France. When Tom Paine pleads for social services for the English workers and (in Professor Raphael's telling words) 'says emphatically . . . that he is speaking of a right and not of charity', then surely what Paine is saying is that the English workers have this right because they have earned it; their efforts have made England rich, and it is unjust that the upper classes should monopolize the nation's wealth.

If we may continue to call these social and economic rights which Babeuf and Tom Paine were claiming the *droits du citoyen*, it may help to make clear that these *droits du citoyen* (in this rather special sense) belong to a logical category which is distinct from that of the *droits de l'homme*, or natural rights, or human rights traditionally (and, as I maintain, correctly) understood as 'political and civil rights' or (in Professor Raphael's term) 'rights of liberty'. First, the *droits du citoyen* are local. Secondly, they are earned: the basis of the claim to them is desert. They are an example of that category of moral rights (mentioned in my original paper, IV in this volume) which are the moral rights of the members of a limited class who have gained their entitlement by some work, service, or status. The *droits de l'homme*, in contrast to this, are not local, they are universal. Furthermore, they are not earned. In a phrase I quoted from Maritain, the *droits de l'homme* are the rights a man has simply because he is human. A man might, I think, be said to disqualify himself from the enjoyment of his human rights; for instance, a man who abuses his liberty may in certain circumstances be justly deprived of his liberty. But a man does not need to qualify to acquire the *droits de l'homme*, as he has to qualify to acquire the *droits du citoyen*. Indeed this is part of what the word 'natural' was meant to intimate by the writers who called the *droits de l'homme* 'natural rights': they were thought of as innate, as part of everyone's birthright as a human being.

Social and economic rights, according to Professor Raphael's account, do not impose duties on all men, but only on some and notably on the governments of States; and although he is critical of my proposed test of practicability, I take it that he would ascribe these duties only to those governments that could be reasonably expected to perform them, and that they would be duties not towards mankind as a whole, but only towards the nationals, *citoyens*, or subjects of those governments. Indeed Professor Raphael makes this point quite clear in that remark of his about the 'responsibility to help people who are in need in other parts of the world', as being a matter of 'benevolence or charity, and not a matter of implementing a right'.

Now I suspect that this remark alone might suffice to prove to those who really believe in 'economic and social rights', as expounded in the United Nations Declaration, that Professor Raphael is not to be numbered among their supporters. He sets out, so it appears, to uphold the 'economic and social rights' against the objections, both philosophical and political, of critics like myself; but what he ends up by defending is the economic and social rights of the inhabitants of countries rich enough to afford to recognize such rights. And if *this* were what was asserted in the United Nations Declaration, that manifesto would take on a very different aspect. Articles 1 to 20, which name the traditional *droits de l'homme*, would still begin with the word 'Everyone ...'. 'Everyone has the right to life, liberty, and security of person', and so on. But Articles 22 to 29, which name the economic and social rights, would no longer begin, as they do now, with the same word 'Everyone . . .'. Instead they would begin with some such expression as 'All persons who live in advanced industrialized communities have the right to social services', and so on. In this case, of course, the manifesto would no longer be presented as a declaration of universal human rights, but as a mixed declaration of universal and non-universal human rights.

I may be asked: why should it not be such? Did not the French Declaration of the Rights of Man and of the Citizen affirm two kinds of right, the general rights of man and the particular rights of Frenchmen? Assuredly, but in that case the double purpose was no drawback, since the Declaration was issued in France, and primarily for the French as part of a conscious programme to revolutionize France. The United Nations Declaration was addressed to the people of the world by the political leaders of the world and presented as a statement of universal human rights, some of those universal rights being of one kind and some of a second kind. My argument — and I am afraid that Professor Raphael's paper has not persuaded me to change my mind — is that the United Nations Declaration is vitiated by a failure to recognize that the economic and social rights are not really a second kind of universal right because they are not universal rights at all; if they are rights in any sense they are local, regional, tribal, or national rights. The United Nations Declaration is ruined by a form of 'category mistake'.

NINE

D. D. RAPHAEL

The Rights of Man and the Rights of the Citizen

I

M Y main purpose in this paper is to reply to the criticisms of my earlier one (V in this volume) made by Mr. Mayo in Essay VI and by Mr. Cranston in Essay VIII. But first I must explain and qualify one of my remarks about Hobbes that is implicitly queried by Professor Macpherson in Essay I.

I wrote on p. 55 that it is a mistake to attribute to Hobbes the view that there is a natural right to life. As Professor Macpherson points out on p. 4 of his paper, Hobbes does speak in *De Corpore Politico* (I, § 1) and in *De Cive* (I, § 8) of a natural right to self-preservation, from which other natural rights follow; since a man has a right to preserve his life, Hobbes says, he must also have a right to do whatever is a necessary means to that end. But in *Leviathan*, where Hobbes had thought out his position more consistently, he does not speak of a natural right to life or self-preservation. Hobbes defines a right as a 'liberty to do or to forbear', and since, on his view, a man will *necessarily* endeavour to preserve his life, the choice implied in 'liberty to do or to forbear' does not arise for self-preservation itself. A man does have a choice in the actions that he performs as means to preserve his life, and therefore the concept of natural right applies to those actions, but not to the end of self-preservation which they promote. So, at the beginning of Chapter 14 of *Leviathan*, Hobbes explicitly defines the Right of Nature as 'the liberty each man hath, to use his own power, as he will himself, for the preservation of his own nature; that is to say, of his own life; and consequently, of doing any thing, which in his own judgement, and reason, he shall conceive to be the aptest means thereunto'.

If one holds, as I do, that Hobbes's conception of natural rights, as rights of action or liberties, is radically different from the traditional conception in which natural rights are rights of recipience, it is of some importance to avoid confusing them. It is important, not only in order to clear our own minds on the use of the concepts, but also in order to understand the positions of the two classical theorists discussed in the first part of this volume. So far as Hobbes is concerned, we fail to appreciate the extent of his originality if we do not see that he is using the terms 'natural right' and 'natural law' in a novel way. In the case of Locke, if we do not distinguish his use from that of Hobbes, we are liable to fall into the error of some of his critics (mainly Idealists) who have said that his talk of natural rights was too individualistic in the sense of being *egoistic*, as in Hobbes. In fact Locke's natural rights (apart from a conflation of the two uses in his natural right to property) are recipient rights, rights against others, corresponding to moral obligations, moral ties between man and man; they are not liberties to do as one pleases. The natural right to life, for example, is not a freedom to preserve one's life, as in Hobbes's earlier statements of his political theory, but an alternative description of the duty of others to refrain from taking one's life.

II

Of course I have been assuming, in the preceding discussion, that there is a genuine difference between rights of action and rights of recipience. But Mr. Mayo (p. 71) challenges this distinction between two senses of the noun 'right', and likewise my consequent distinction between a right to act and a right to be allowed to act. As Mr. Mayo realizes, the first distinction is not peculiar to me. I invented the labels, 'rights of action' and 'rights of recipience', in my book *Moral Judgement*, but lawyers have traditionally drawn the distinction by calling the first 'liberties'. While Mr. Mayo notes Professor Hart's use of the distinction in this form, Professor Hart himself was well aware that he was simply repeating a juristic commonplace. Whether or not Hobbes was explicitly conscious of two different senses of 'a right', Pufendorf undoubtedly was. In Book III, Chapter 5, § 1, of *De Jure Naturae et Gentium*, Pufendorf distinguishes between the use of 'a right' (1) as *facultas et competentia ad aliquid habendum,* to which, he says, there must always correspond some obligation on the part of another person, and (2) as *facultas ad aliquid agendum,* to which there does not always correspond an obligation of another.

Although Mr. Mayo says (p. 70) that his first disagreement with me is a serious one, I am not clear just what he is disagreeing about. I said that we use the expression 'a right' in two senses. I did not say that we *always* find it natural to speak of a right to do X when X is not wrong. On the contrary, I said (p. 57) that we do not normally use the expression unless we are also claiming a recipient right to non-interference. I argued, however, against Carritt, that when we do speak, in such circumstances, of a right to act, we are making two claims, not one. Mr. Mayo allows (p. 71) that an expression of the form 'A has a right to do X' has come to do 'double duty', and although his aetiology of the process strikes me as artificial, the final result seems to coincide with my contention. Nevertheless Mr. Mayo says earlier (p. 71) that he rejects my distinction between rights of action and rights of recipience, and in particular the 'awkward' distinction between rights to act and rights to be allowed to act.

In support of the first rejection, he argues that affirmative cases (i.e., saying one has a right, as contrasted with saying one has no right) show up the difference in meaning between a statement that an act is not wrong and a statement that one has a right to do it. He gives the example of a cynical adulterer, who might be ready to say sincerely that his seduction of another man's wife was not wrong, but who would, in that event, be very far from saying that he had a right to seduce her. I have little experience of how cynical adulterers are prepared to use moral terms concerning their seductions, and I do not think that the understanding of moral language is much assisted by offering, as a sole example, the imaginary replies of one who is, *ex hypothesi, cynical* about the moral issue raised. Still, if we are to indulge in flights of imagination, I imagine that Don Juan, if asked whether he thought he had a right to seduce other men's wives, would say: 'I have a right to seduce any woman. For me, women exist simply for that purpose.'

In support of the second rejection (of the distinction between a right to act and a right to be allowed to act), Mr. Mayo says that I have gone wrong by giving an example which differs significantly from the one given by Carritt. My example was 'You have no right to kick the boy'; Carritt's was 'You have no right to enter': and the significant difference is that entering is, without further specification, morally neutral, while kicking a person is, without further specification, morally wrong. But this is beside the point. One who says 'You have no right to enter' is adding a specification of a moral or legal character to the act of entering in the particular circumstances. Mr. Mayo's argument does not affect my criticism of Carritt's analysis of the statement. Carritt held that 'You have no right to enter' is simply equivalent to 'Nobody is obliged to refrain from preventing your entry'. The error of Carritt's analysis can be seen from the fact that it makes sense to say 'You have no right to enter, and therefore others are entitled to prevent you'. The second clause of this statement is a consequence, not a repetition, of the first clause.

Mr. Mayo says (p. 71) that what I call a right of action is merely a matter of idiom. I do not think I have ever suggested that it was anything else. I stated that '*A* has a right to do *X*' is an alternative way of saying '*A* has no obligation to refrain from doing *X*'; it is a way of expressing the absence of obligation. My substantial point was that this use of the noun 'right' should not be confused with the use in which a right on the part of one person implies the presence of an obligation on the part of some other person or persons. It is worth noting, incidentally, that the 'matter of idiom' is not peculiar to English and is therefore unlikely to depend simply on the existence or non-existence, in the English language, of 'convenient locutions' or of 'circumlocutions' for expressing adverse or non-adverse judgements on actions. The French, I think, are more ready than we are to speak of having, or not having, 'the right' to do something when all that is meant is that one may, or that one ought not, to do it. The French language in fact has the two phrases, '*le droit de*' and '*le droit à*', which seem to indicate a tendency to mark in words the distinction between rights of action and rights of recipience. The correspondence is not complete, for '*droit de*' is normally used before a verb, and '*droit à*' before a noun, so that one would speak of *le droit de recevoir quelque chose* as well as of *le droit de faire quelque chose*. Yet the distinction in usage is not the purely grammatical one of allotting '*droit de*' to verbs and '*droit à*' to nouns.

'*Droit de*' is sometimes used before a noun, e.g., '*droit de grâce*' (the right or privilege of pardon), '*droit de vie et de mort*' (the right or authority to decide whether a man should live or die), '*droit de cité*' (the freedom of a city), '*droit de visite*' (the right of search). All these are examples of rights of action, and it seems to me that French idiom tends to confirm that this use of the noun 'right' expresses a different concept from that of a recipient right.

Mr. Mayo next says (p. 72) that I go 'even further astray' when I make a right to freedom from interference depend upon having a right of action. I said that a man has a right to non-interference only when his action is not wrong or unlawful. Mr. Mayo thinks it is 'totally unacceptable' to suggest that a man never has a right to freedom from interference in morally wrong (he says 'immoral') conduct. That depends on what one takes to constitute morally wrong conduct. I should not call an action morally wrong unless, as one (though not the only) condition, it is contrary to the interests of some other person or persons, and I cannot see anything objectionable in saying of *such* action, if there are no countervailing considerations (as of course there may be), that the agent has no right to freedom from interference, i.e., that others *may* interfere. This, I need hardly add, is not to say that others *ought* to interfere, and I imagine that Mr. Mayo just made a slip when he wrote (p. 72) that my view implies that 'a person engaging in immoral conduct of whatever kind ought always to be interfered with'.

Mr. Mayo is likewise mistaken in supposing (p. 72) that on this point I have fallaciously derived a 'substantive moral conclusion . . . from a conceptual analysis of what a right is'. The substantive moral conclusion, 'It is permissible (in the absence of countervailing considerations) for others to interfere with action that is wrong', follows from (being simply an explication of) the equally substantive moral premise, 'A man who has no right to act has no recipient right to non-interference'. When I expressed the view (p. 56) that a man has a right to freedom from interference if, and only if, he has a right of action, I was not pretending to derive this moral assertion from the analysis of concepts. Acceptance of my analytic distinction between the two kinds of rights leaves it logically possible to differ from my opinion about a substantive moral connexion and to say, either that a right to non-interference does not necessarily presuppose a right of action, or that a right of action does not necessarily imply a right to non-interference. The first of these two positions might be taken by an extreme anarchist, who could say that there is always a right to non-interference with whatever one chooses to do. The second position might possibly be taken by my imaginary Don Juan, and would undoubtedly be taken by Hobbes in regard to the state of nature: Don Juan (who illustrates the Hobbesian natural man in one respect) might say that while he had a right (of action) to seduce any woman, he had no right (of recipience) that others should refrain from trying to stop him; and Hobbes would say that while a man in the state of nature has the right (of action) to do whatever he thinks fit for self-preservation, he has no rights of recipience at all (i.e., others have no obligations towards him) prior to the making of covenants.

III

I turn now to the distinction, within recipient rights, between rights to liberty on the one hand and rights to 'opportunity or more than opportunity' on the other. I agree with Mr. Mayo (pp. 70–1) that the first shades into the second, and that it is nevertheless important to distinguish the two ends of the spectrum. When I wrote of 'opportunity or more than opportunity', this did not 'betray an uneasiness', as Mr. Mayo thinks, but was rather a brief indication of the point which he has brought out more fully and more clearly. It seems to me that Mr. Cranston gives a similar indication in regard to the political right to take part in government, which forms the subject of Article 21 of the Universal Declaration. In Essay IV (p. 46) Mr. Cranston couples this with the new economic and social rights, and in Essay VIII he evidently agrees with me in including this right to participate in government among 'the rights of the citizen' as contrasted with 'the rights of man' described in Articles 1 to 20. But I notice that on p. 99, when he says that only Articles 1 to 20 legitimately begin with the word 'Everyone', he goes on to say that Articles 22 to 29 need to be qualified in this respect. Here he omits mention of Article 21. I take it this is because he is not quite sure whether to say (in accordance with the Liberalism of the classical natural rights theorists) that the democratic right of participation in government should be demanded for everyone, or alternatively (in accordance with the realism which he advocates in both his papers) that such a demand, being merely an aspiration in the present state of world politics, should be left out of a sensible universal declaration. Whatever Mr. Cranston's view may be, however, I agree with Mr. Mayo that no fixed lines, valid for past, present, and future alike, can be drawn on his spectrum, and that the lines that are drawn from time to time depend on historical circumstances. The right to participate in government, which is today a right of the citizen (or, as Mr. Cranston would say, a local right), may become in the future a right of man (or at least a right of the citizen of the world) if and when there should be a world government. It is still open to debate whether a right which today can only be a right of the national citizen should be included in the Universal Declaration as a moral right that all men have in relation to their own national societies.

At this point I should like to insert a comment on the expressions 'civil rights' and 'political rights'. Mr. Cranston tells us (p. 46) that, in the discussion of draft conventions, the rights set out in Articles 1 to 20 of the Universal Declaration have been called 'political and civil rights', while those described in the later Articles are called 'economic and social rights'. It would, I think, be clearer to reserve the name of 'political' for the right to take part in government that is specified in Article 21. Some, if not all, of the rights included in the earlier Articles have traditionally been called 'civil rights', but I think that this name too is rather misleading, for most of these rights do not pertain only to the citizens of a State. In the positive law of civilized countries, foreigners as well as citizens are entitled to legal protection of life, liberty, and security of person, to freedom from enslavement, torture, and arbitrary arrest, to a fair hearing and the initial presumption of innocence if charged with a penal offence, and so on. This is why I have preferred to speak of these rights as 'rights of liberty' rather than as 'civil rights'. If furthermore, as Mr. Cranston and I both maintain, these are all, as 'rights of man', to be contrasted with political, economic, and social rights as 'rights of the citizen', it would be particularly confusing to use the adjective 'civil' of the former.

I shall leave aside for the present Mr. Cranston's dispute with me on the question whether the rights of the citizen can be called universal in any sense. Here I shall just say that I entirely agree with him when he describes my position as nearer to his own than to that which he attacked in the first place. Mr. Mayo, however, rejects my distinction between the rights of man and the rights of the citizen. Indeed he wants 'to invert [my] order of conceptual priority' and to make what I call the rights of the citizen 'the prime ingredient in a typical list of human rights' (pp. 77–8).

I agree with Mr. Mayo's view (p. 77) that declarations of human rights are made in order to secure *action* (or inaction) *by governments*. This emphasizes something that I did not make sufficiently clear. But I do not agree that the rights themselves are *all* claims *against* governments, as Mr. Mayo maintains on p. 78. I wrote in my earlier paper (p. 62) that rights of liberty are 'rights to be left in peace *by other men and by governments*' (except in so far as governments intervene in order to keep the peace and preserve liberties). The American Declaration of Independence says: 'We hold these truths to be self-evident, that all men . . . are endowed . . . with certain unalienable Rights, that among these are Life, Liberty, and the pursuit of Happiness. That to secure these rights, Governments are instituted among Men. . . .' If government is instituted *to secure* the rights to life and liberty, these rights cannot be simply rights *against* the government. The French Declaration of 1789 carries the same implication when it says that the purpose of all political association is the preservation of the rights of man. The Preamble to the Universal Declaration of Human Rights speaks of the necessity 'that human rights should be protected by the rule of law', thereby implying that the rights themselves exist apart from the need or claim for State action to protect them. The Universal Declaration does not in fact address itself to governments alone, but appeals to 'every individual and every organ of society . . . to promote respect for these rights and freedoms and by progressive measures, national and international, to secure their universal and effective recognition and observance, both among the peoples of Member States themselves and among the peoples of territories under their jurisdiction'.

Mr. Mayo thinks (p. 77) that when a declaration mentions the right to life, it is simply claiming freedom from arbitrary execution by a government, and is not also claiming that the government should have effective laws against homicide. This is not the view of Locke, reflected in the American Declaration and thereby in the later declarations. In Chapter 2 of the *Second Treatise*, Locke describes his natural rights by saying the law of nature requires that 'no one ought to harm another in his life, health, liberty, or possessions', and he then goes on to speak of murder being punishable by death. Similarly Adam Smith in the following century, at the beginning of his Lectures on Jurisprudence, takes it for granted as a commonplace that the natural right to life calls for laws against homicide and personal injury as part of the first business of any government.[1] Mr. Mayo compares the moral right not to be killed with the moral right not to be deceived, which admittedly has no place in the declarations. But there is a difference. The right not to be deceived does not appear in declarations of human rights for the same reason that it does not appear in positive law, namely because it is unenforceable. There are other moral rights and obligations which do appear in positive law but not in declarations of human rights, e.g., the rights and obligations of contract. Declarations of human rights are selective, partly for the reasons given by Mr. Cranston. They select what is practicable and what is of paramount importance. The selection is also guided, as Mr. Mayo says, by what has been historically significant.

If we now agree that the older rights of liberty are not only claims against arbitrary action by a government, but are also claims against individuals, which the government is asked to protect, can we accept Mr. Mayo's view (p. 77) that it is the political, economic, and social rights with which governments are 'mostly' concerned? The primary task of any government is to give *security* to those who come under its jurisdiction, security of life, liberty, and property, as Locke said. The granting to all citizens of the facility to participate in government takes place only in a democracy, and the legal provision of economic and social rights has received general acknowledgement as a function of government only in very recent times.

While I grant, therefore, that declarations of human rights are addressed chiefly to governments, I still maintain that the Lockean rights of liberty are fundamental. I also maintain my distinction between them, as rights of man, and the others, as rights of the citizen. A government is expected to secure the rights of liberty for every person living within its jurisdiction, not just for citizens. Foreigners have both

110 O	D. D. Raphael

the rights and the obligations relating to homicide and the rest. But they do not have the right to vote, and it would not be thought wrong if they were excluded from the right to social security (except in so far as they are parties to a contractual and contributory scheme).

IV

Mr. Mayo adds some puzzling remarks about conceptual analysis in relation to historical facts. Having properly noted that the content of a declaration of rights is affected by history, he challenges my distinction between the rights of man and the rights of the citizen on the ground that 'analysis of concepts, with which [I "profess"] to have been concerned, cannot wait on the facts of political history' (p. 78). I do not understand why Mr. Mayo supposes that the changing facts of history are irrelevant to the analysis of concepts. Does he think that the concepts used by men are eternal and immutable? Many concepts are liable to change as the result of historical change, and political concepts more than most. Would Mr. Mayo say, for example, that men's understanding and use of the concept of sovereignty has been unaffected by history? Certainly the analysis of concepts does not need to *wait* upon historical facts, but it does need to take account of them and to adapt itself to them.

I wrote (on p. 66) that 'since there is no World State, it makes no sense to speak of a right to participate in the government of mankind as a whole'. I meant that it makes no sense now. If a world government comes into existence in the future, it will make sense then. Mr. Mayo thinks (p. 78) that the historical fact that there is not now a world government 'cannot possibly make the difference between the right of participation in government being, or not being, a human right', and he goes on to say that the Universal Declaration 'virtually announces a right to world government'. I do not think the last statement is correct. Article 28 of the Universal Declaration says: 'Everyone is entitled to a social and international order in which the rights and freedoms set forth in this Declaration can be fully realized.' An international *order* is not necessarily a world government. There is no world government now, and there is not likely to be one for a long time to come, but there is an international order — less secure than it might be, though more secure than appears at first sight. But in any event, if a world government is established in the future, this will mean that one form of citizenship will be world-wide, and in consequence some of the rights of the citizen will then, *as a matter of historical fact*, become universal in the stronger sense of that term, because one form of citizenship will be, *as a matter of historical fact*, world-wide. It will not be simply because all men have the natural qualities that Mr. Mayo refers to (on pp. 68–9) as the foundation of the rights of man.

However, when I spoke of 'the analysis of concepts' in the last sentence of my earlier paper (p. 67), I was using the expression rather loosely. I was simply contrasting the taking of a definite stand on a practical political issue with the task of elucidating distinctions that may *indirectly* help, in a minor way, towards the reaching of a practical decision, such as the decision whether to try to incorporate economic and social rights, as well as the rights of liberty, in an international convention. I do not much care whether my distinction is to be called a distinction between two concepts or a distinction in the application of a single concept. My concern was to see whether a theoretical discussion, by drawing distinctions (whether they be called conceptual or not), could be of some assistance on the practical issue. I think it can. It can show, for instance, *why* it is more difficult to give legal effect to the later group of rights, but it can also show that this is not impossible. The older machinery of law for dealing with crimes and torts cannot be applied to the protection of economic and social rights, just because these rights correspond, not to the duties of individuals, but to the duties of governments. The kind of law that is needed is the law of social administration, not the law of crimes and torts, in which individuals are liable to be charged or sued.

V

My disagreement with Mr. Cranston is narrower than with Mr. Mayo. I have already accepted Mr. Cranston's statement that my position is nearer to his own than to that of many who class economic and social rights together with the rights of liberty as human rights. Nevertheless I suggested that the rights of the citizen could be called universal rights, not in the strong sense that they are rights of all men against all men, but in the weaker sense that they are rights possessed by all men though not necessarily against all men. Mr. Cranston criticizes this contention on two counts.

In the first place, Mr. Cranston argues (p. 97), economic and social rights are not universal at all, because they are *'enjoyed* by some men only'. I am not sure how to take the word 'enjoyed'. On the one hand, Mr. Cranston may mean that only some groups of men in fact receive things like social security. That is true but, I think, irrelevant. In his earlier paper, on p. 49, when explaining the difference between moral rights and legal rights, Mr. Cranston said: 'Not all my moral rights may in fact be enjoyed. . . . So just as the crucial question with legal rights is "Are they secured and enjoyed?", the crucial question in a moral right is "Is there a just title?" Is there a sound moral claim? *Justification* is the central question.' I agree with that, and of course Mr. Cranston went on to say, on p. 49, that 'human rights are a form of moral right'. On the other hand, Mr. Cranston may be using the word 'enjoyed' in his second paper to mean simply 'held as rights'. For he proceeds to elaborate his statement that economic and social rights are enjoyed by some men only, with the explanation that, according to my account, these rights are 'local rights', rights within a political community. This is undoubtedly in accordance with what I wrote, but I do not see that it prevents such rights from being universal in the weaker sense. I said that if we help people who are in need in other parts of the world, our action is one of benevolence or charity and not one of implementing a right, so that I certainly agree that a destitute person in India does not have a right to be helped by a benefactor in Britain. At the same time, however, I implied that the destitute person in India has a right against his own government as representing the people of India. His right can be called a local right, since it is a right against a local group only. But that does not prevent it from being a universal right in the weaker sense, if it is a right that every man has against the members of the local political community to which he belongs. In short, the latter part of Mr. Cranston's argument on this score merely establishes what I allowed from the start, namely that these rights are not universal rights in the stronger sense, i.e., rights of all men *against all men*. Mr. Cranston would still want to challenge me on practicability, but that is a different question, to which I shall return later. My point at the moment is that Mr. Cranston, so far as I can see, has not shown that my universal rights in the weaker sense are, simply by being 'local rights', not universal rights at all.

Mr. Cranston's second argument is more important and raises a fundamental issue about the basis of rights. He maintains that the rights of the citizen, in addition to being local, are based on desert (p. 98). I wish to argue that they can also be based on need together with the concept of fraternity (or social responsibility). Mr. Cranston tells us that Babeuf, and suggests that Tom Paine, thought of economic and social rights in terms of desert. I think there is evidence for this view of Paine, but Babeuf seems to me to strike a different note.

My earlier reference to Babeuf in Essay V (p. 62) did not concern property, as Mr. Cranston's exposition does (p. 98), but the right to education (and the obligation to work). The *Manifeste des Égaux* states that there should be a common education (and a common supply of food) for all, because all have the same needs and faculties, while the *Analyse de la Doctrine de Babeuf* speaks in similar vein of education as necessary for a man's happiness. That is to say, the right to education, like the rights of liberty, is founded on the universal human capacity and need for self-fulfilment. So far as property is concerned, the general tenor of Babeuf's thesis is that land ought to be held in common and its fruits distributed equally. And while he speaks, in an essay that he quotes at his trial,[2] of the justice of taking back property from those 'who have more than their individual due of society's goods', on the ground that they have stolen it, he still makes the original right to equal distribution depend on need, and emphatically not on desert in terms of industry or ability. In fact he describes distinctions of merit as 'murderous folly'.

On Tom Paine, Mr. Cranston has a better case. When Paine speaks, in *The Rights of Man*,[3] of old-age pensions as a right and not a charity, he supports the claim on the ground that the proposed payments are little more than the legal interest on the taxes that have been contributed by everyone, on average, in England. On the other hand, in *Agrarian Justice*, where he repeatedly stresses that he is talking of a right and not a charity, of justice and not bounty, he argues for this conclusion on two different grounds. First, he refers to the original natural right of everyone to a share of land in its natural state (though, unlike Babeuf, he is ready to acknowledge also the right of the possessor to the additional value introduced by cultivation), and to a consequent right of non-owners of land to be indemnified for dispossession.[4] Secondly, he regards the moral offensiveness of affluence joined with wretchedness in a single society as being itself an affront to justice.[5] On the latter point, Paine's view seems to be that affluent individuals have a duty of charity to succour the distressed, but that the scale of the problem requires national action and that this is what turns the requirement of charity into one of justice. In this thought, as in the kind of plan he proposes, Paine comes close to the modern concept of the Welfare State.

Mr. Cranston's point of view can be more firmly illustrated from a third example of an eighteenth-century writer, Daines Barrington, a hard-headed lawyer, not a radical political theorist. The passage I shall quote is of interest for the history of the idea of economic and social rights, both because it is itself earlier (1769) than the other eighteenth-century writings to which Professor Friedrich and I have referred, and because it is a comment on the Elizabethan Poor Law of 1601. That statute, says Barrington, is founded upon two principles. 'The principles are, *that every one capable of working shall be employed; and that he who is incapable, shall be relieved and supported by the parish.* It should seem therefore that a day-labourer, who hath been industrious whilst his health and strength permitted, hath as much right, when weakened by old age or sickness, to a certain support, as the worn-out soldier has to his Chelsea, or seaman to his Greenwich.'[6] Barrington goes on to praise the law of England for treating as a matter of obligation what is elsewhere charity, and for having not only made the poor free but also 'provided a certain and solid establishment, to prevent their necessities and indigence'.[7] Here the meeting of needs is classed with liberty, and is described as 'a matter of obligation and necessity', but in his explicit use of the term 'right' Barrington appeals to desert.

What should we say today? Are we to maintain that a *right* to a minimum subsistence exists only if it is earned? Suppose a man has been a chronic invalid from childhood. Presumably we shall all agree that the more fortunate members of his society (or the government on their behalf) have a duty to provide him with what he needs for a tolerable existence. The question is whether we should also say that he has a right to such assistance. I for one wish to say that he has. I think that rights can be based on need (or on capacity) as well as on desert. Mr. Cranston would doubtless agree that this is true of some rights, the rights of liberty at least, for he grounds these not on desert but on the mere fact that one is human. Now one cannot exercise the initiative of a human being (which is what the rights of liberty are intended to protect), or indeed remain a human being at all, unless the basic needs of life are satisfied; and if a man is not in a position to do this for himself, it seems to me reasonable to say that he has a right, as a human being, to the assistance of others in meeting these needs — subject of course to practicability, which is a reason for confining the area of such rights to the political community.

I say that he has this right as a human being, and I would maintain similarly that it is the human capacity to think and to choose that gives men the political right to share in government. I would not agree with Mr. Cranston that a man has to qualify for the rights of the citizen, if this means that he has to earn them. It is true that a State is not normally willing to grant citizenship automatically to aliens who come to live within its borders, i.e., to those who may be presumed to possess already the citizenship of another State, but it is a mark of a civilized State to confer citizenship automatically upon all who are born within its borders (notwithstanding some exceptions in States that purport to be civilized). One does not therefore need any special qualification to become a citizen of *a* State, though place of birth (or parentage) determines, as a matter of convenience, *which* State it is to be. The precautions taken by a State before granting its own citizenship to persons who are, or have been, citizens of another State can of course be explained in terms of international relations and are no objection to the general validity of the thesis that the privileges (and obligations) of citizenship fall to be acquired by men in virtue of common human qualities together with the fact that the whole of the inhabited world in modern times is divided up into States.

My view is, then, that the rights of the citizen are human rights in that, like the rights of liberty, they are based upon human qualities and the human condition. I distinguish them from the original 'rights of man' simply because the 'rights of man' are universal in the strong sense, rights against all men. It is practicability that determines whether a particular set of rights belongs to the one category or the other. The criminal and civil law of any State can give to the alien, as easily as to the citizen, protection of life, liberty, and possessions, and consequently a man is morally entitled to such protection from interference by others wherever he may be. Political rights are confined to citizens for reasons of convenience and of national security. Economic and social rights are in many countries similarly confined because it is thought that a wider application would be economically or politically unacceptable.

VI

In saying that need or capacity can give rise to rights, one has to be careful where to draw the line. It is only too easy, as Mr. Cranston says, to include all manner of aspirations within the category of rights and thereby to reduce a practicable set of precepts, that may be given legal effect, into a vision of pie in the sky. I remember that when we first discussed this issue at the Sixth World Congress of the International Political Science Association, M. Bertrand de Jouvenel supported Mr. Cranston's view with an apt illustration of the ease with which one can extend the notion of rights as needs. He began like this: 'Every child needs a garden; and since he needs it, we can say he has a right to it. Further, since in "the state of nature" the whole world was a garden, the right of every child to a garden is pre-eminently a "natural right".' Mr. Cranston does well to insist on adding the tests of practicability and paramount importance to universality. A need comes to be called a right only when it is generally recognized to be of paramount importance (as the need for basic subsistence is) and when the meeting of it is practicable.

The fact is, however, as Professor Schneider reminds us in Essay VII, that the scope of human rights has gradually widened. This process has gone hand in hand with an increase both of the sense of social responsibility and of economic improvement. Whereas in the eighteenth century only a few men were ready to think of rights arising from need as such, this conception is now generally accepted in the idea of the Welfare State. And while Mr. Cranston is justified in repeating that many countries do not have the economic resources for a scheme of social security such as now exists in more affluent societies, the experience of the International Labour Office shows that even underdeveloped countries can often make some sort of minimum provision if they learn the know-how of social administration.

The gradual extension of the scope of rights means that the concept of justice gradually takes over more of what formerly came under the concept of charity. Legal or State action is called in to deal with what was previously left to voluntary or individual action. Certain conditions have to be satisfied before this change is appropriate, just as there are conditions for making harmful conduct subject to criminal law. In the latter case the conditions are, first, that the harm to be controlled is serious (or, although not serious in particular instances, is liable to be so widespread as to become a public nuisance beyond control by private action or mere social disapproval); and secondly, that control by the 'rough engine' (as Sir James Stephen called it) of the criminal law is practicable. In the former case the conditions are, first, an awakening of the general social conscience (not just the conscience of isolated individuals) to the duty of fraternity to succour the needy, together with a recognition of Tom Paine's point that voluntary action cannot suffice to relieve widespread misery; and secondly, practicability again, in terms both of economics and of administration. When these conditions are satisfied, the idea of charity tends to be replaced by that of justice, i.e., by plans for legal action with the notion of rights corresponding to communal obligation.

Mr. Mayo, in his interesting discussion of the doctrine that rights and duties are correlative, allows (p. 74) that it is natural for the use of the term 'rights' to be extended beyond undertakings, but he deplores a deliberate extension by theorists, who, he thinks, are concerned simply to maintain the correlativity thesis. I suggest that some theorists, in making the extension, are more concerned to extend at the same time the application of the idea of 'perfect' obligation, as it is used of undertakings. Mr. Mayo himself notes the persistent tendency in political theory to look on organized society as involving an undertaking. I think that the extension of legal ideas to moral duties is often made in order to strengthen the ties of social morality. This means that what purports to be an analysis of concepts as they are now used, is in fact a proposal for modifying usage; or perhaps rather it is an explicit indication of change that is already taking place implicitly, and a method of hastening that change by bringing it out clearly.

Such a practical concern, going along with the clarification of concepts, is quite characteristic of social and political philosophy. It is to be found in almost all political philosophies of any consequence, and their philosophical character is none the worse for it, in my opinion, so long as they are subject to the continual criticism which is the hallmark of philosophy. At any rate that is how I see the debate in this volume on theoretical issues about human rights. We have tried to clarify, and to justify or criticize, various distinctions. In doing so we have, I hope, made a small contribution towards understanding some of the problems that face the translation of theory into practice.

TEN

J. E. S. FAWCETT

The International Protection
of Human Rights

I

THE international protection of human rights[1] is not simply an ideal objective; it is a necessary condition. When Abraham Lincoln said that, if we grant freedom to the slave, we assure freedom to the free, he showed with deep insight that liberty cannot be partitioned in a community, and that a systematic denial of the rights of some leads ineluctably to the diminution of liberty for all. For this denial in one part of the community means an increase of uncontrolled power in another, and the wider the denial the greater will be the concentration of that power. But no country is an island. Such power comes to threaten the life of other communities when, as has often happened, it seeks to maintain itself by expansion. Again, humanity, for all its varieties and divisions, is like a 'field' of physical theory, through which some forces can move with great rapidity, creating or releasing strains; and so the denial in Africa of what are thought of as common rights can cause tension and insecurity in New York or London. But there are few countries in which there are not people, and even governments, endeavouring to advance and improve the condition of human rights, and such governments may sometimes actually welcome international supervision or control of human rights, since this may help to remove domestic opposition to reform. Finally, the reduction of fundamental rights to short, comprehensible, common formulae makes them known, talked about, and adaptable to political uses, so that slowly opinion is formed and policy influenced across frontiers.

II

What are these common, natural rights, which call for international protection? They have been shaped by social forces: the polarities between the individual and the State, between workers and employers, between peoples of different languages and colour, between authority and freedom in religion, between men and women. They have been shaped too by intellectual efforts over two thousand years, often changing direction or broken off but never abandoned, to discover or construct a law of nature.[2]

It is for the historian and political theorist to appreciate correctly the interaction between these forces and the means of resolving conflicts between them; but there is place here for a description of some of the sources of the ideas, both of the nature of human rights and of how they are to be implemented, which have been generalized in the Declarations and Conventions of the last twenty years.

Slavery   In the abolition of slavery, international action was the prime mover, since the elimination of the slave trade across the seas, in which Great Britain was the leader, long preceded the abolition of slave-owning in many countries, including British territories. While a slave went free on landing in Great Britain,[3] the institution of slavery was not abolished in its overseas territories until 1834; and in a celebrated case in 1817,[4] Lord Stowell reversed the condemnation by the Vice-Admiralty Court of Sierra Leone of a French vessel carrying slaves, on the ground that neither slavery nor engaging in the slave trade had yet been made unlawful in France. He recognized that, though a Declaration against the slave trade had been adopted at the Congress of Vienna in 1815, it had been left to the participating countries to give effect to it through national legislation. It was not till 1831 that France conceded the right of visit and search of its vessels suspected of slave-trading; and though Great Britain reached agreement with the United States in 1814 on the principle of suppression of the traffic in slaves, it was only in 1862 that visit and search on the high seas was established between them. But after the great change in the United States, slavery, in the sense of men and women being owned as chattels, was largely confined to regions of Africa and Asia, from which it is still not wholly eradicated. The Berlin Conference in 1885 forbade the use of the Congo territory for the marketing or transit of slaves, and the Brussels Conference of 1890, in order to deal with the slave trade in and around the Red Sea, introduced an extensive system of control over land routes and at ports, in which Persia, Zanzibar, and the Congo territory joined.[5]

Forced Labour   But other forms of servitude, in particular forced labour and the traffic in women, called for international attention. Conventions in 1904 and 1910, in which sixteen States participated, provided that national legislation should make 'white slavery' a criminal offence, that is, the procuring of women for prostitution abroad, by fraud or duress in cases of those over twenty years of age. But legislation came slowly and in 1921 the League of Nations tackled the problem afresh with a new Convention, referring significantly to 'treatment of women', without qualification of colour. Enlarged in 1933, this Convention was redrafted in 1949, being widened to cover exploitation of prostitutes even with their consent.

Forced labour, for the great part in mandated and other dependent territories, was a concern of the League and the International Labour Office from their foundation. The I.L.O. sponsored two major Conventions in 1930 and 1957, which have gone far to define the limits of forced or compulsory labour. That of 1930, recognizing the economic difficulties for some countries of its peremptory abolition, permitted its use for a transitional period, for public purposes only and subject to certain guarantees set out in the Convention. That of 1957 sought to limit the punitive use of forced labour. While it is generally accepted that compulsory labour is permissible for convicts serving sentence, the Convention called for 'the suppression and non-use of any form of forced or compulsory labour . . . as a means of political coercion or education, or as a punishment for holding or expressing political or ideological views opposed to the established political, social or economic system . . . [or] as a means of labour discipline, as a punishment for having participated in strikes, or as a means of racial, social, national or religious discrimination'. It is to be noted that, while over seventy countries are parties to the first Convention, many fewer are parties to the second. A notable absentee from both is the United States, which observed of the second Convention that 'it is inappropriate to embody

I   R.P.T.

in an international draft treaty provisions governing the relationship of
an individual to his own government', but that it had voted in favour
of the Convention and would voluntarily submit the reports called for
by it.

Conditions of Labour   But the I.L.O. pushed forward over a
much wider field. The League Covenant[6] called on members of the
League to 'endeavour to secure and maintain fair and humane conditions of labour for men, women and children, both in their own
countries and in all countries to which their commercial and industrial
relations extend, and for that purpose will establish and maintain the
necessary international organizations'. The I.L.O. has sponsored over
a hundred Conventions[7] on the conditions of labour, industrial, agri-
cultural, and maritime. The effectiveness of these Conventions rests in
part on economic forces: pressure from trade unions for the enforcement of the various principles they contain, and the unwillingness of
other countries to acquiesce in the conditions of unfair trade competition created by a country failing to accept or observe them.[8] The I.L.O.
has also established means of administering the Conventions, through
systems of reports or complaints.

Diplomatic Protection   Another factor in the development of
human rights has been the practice of States in protecting their nationals
from ill-treatment or exploitation abroad. A long line of treaties
between States has enabled the nationals of one to go to the territory
of another, and reside and do business there, with the expectation of
fair treatment from public authority, whether executive or judicial.[9]
Further, States have for centuries exercised the right of protection of
their nationals by reprisals, diplomatic intervention, and recourse to
arbitration, and out of this has grown a great corpus of principles and
detailed rules. Among these principles governing the treatment of
foreigners a few words will be devoted to four: a minimum standard of
treatment; no taking of property without just compensation; no denial
of justice; and the right of asylum.

Many of the treaties of establishment, as they are called, offer
national treatment; that is to say, a national of one contracting State
will be accorded in the other, in a number of prescribed ways (residence,

taxation, licence to engage in a particular trade or business, and so on), treatment no less favourable than that given to local nationals. But suppose the State administration treats its own nationals badly? Out of such situations grew the principle that even 'national treatment' of a foreigner is not acceptable if it falls below a minimum standard. This standard is close to the notion of fundamental rights.

By denial of justice is meant in this context either the denial of access to the courts, including the absence of any remedy in law against arbitrary actions by the Executive, or some abuse or unfairness in court proceedings themselves.

Although the modalities of compensation for the taking of property in the public interest are often a matter of dispute, the principle that some compensation is payable has had a long history of application and is still generally accepted.[10]

The grant of asylum to political fugitives has formed an essential part of extradition practice, and has taken the form in some countries, such as France, of the creation of a recognized status of 'political refugee', and the principle has been embodied in more than one Convention.[11]

But a State against which complaint is made under one or more of these principles is also protected by a well-established rule that, before it is bound to meet such an international claim, it must be given an opportunity, within its own legal system, to redress the wrong alleged to have been done. The individual concerned must therefore first exhaust all local remedies that are effective and available to him for the wrong, before an international claim can be made on his behalf.

Self-Determination   The status and protection of characteristic groups, forming part of larger communities or societies of their own, have long been of international concern. These groups may differ markedly from the rest of the community in language, religion, or culture, or in being technically undeveloped, or primitive in their social organization in comparison to it or to the outside world, and out of these relations arise strains. International law, drawn so much from European civilization, began with the exclusion from the pale of law of peoples outside the circle of Christian Europe. Grotius approved discrimination against non-Christian States, and it was not till 1856 that the Ottoman Empire was formally admitted to 'participate in the public law and concert of Europe'. Again the innumerable 'treaties' that were concluded mainly in Africa and Asia between the great trading companies, or even governments, and local communities were rigorously denied the status of international agreements, the communities not being persons known to the law. But such agreements were regarded as not the less obligatory and were sometimes, as for example with the indigenous Indians in Canada and the United States, given statutory force. This sense of obligation to, and indeed responsibility for, weaker peoples, was carried over into the mandate system of the League. Article 22(1) of the Covenant said:

> To those colonies and territories which as a consequence of the late war have ceased to be under the sovereignty of the States which formerly governed them and which are inhabited by peoples not yet able to stand by themselves under the strenuous conditions of the modern world, there should be applied the principle that the well-being and development of such peoples form a sacred trust of civilization and that securities for the performance of this trust should be embodied in this Covenant.

But independence was not set as the necessary goal of the mandate system;[12] and the supervision of the mandated territories by the League Council, with the help of the Permanent Mandates Commission (an independent and expert body), was not in advance of the general thinking of the time on colonial administration. Good administration and judicious social progress, rather than a drive for independence, also formed the main desiderata of the U.N. Charter for non-self-governing territories generally and trust territories in particular, and independence was hedged around with conditions, and still had no fixed goal in time.[13] But the independence movement, accelerated after 1945 far beyond any expectation, produced sixty or more new States in twenty years, and those that had been once uncivilized, then backward, then underdeveloped, were at last equal and developing countries. In December 1960 the United Nations made the self-determination of peoples a matter of political obligation.[14]

Minorities   A group within a community may be a minority in terms of numbers, or of power, or of both. The history of the Christian minorities in the Ottoman Empire, of Greece and Macedonia, the Low Countries, Eastern Silesia, and, in the last two decades, of India, Palestine, Cyprus, North Africa, British Guiana, Malaysia, and Rhodesia, is filled with efforts, by means of constitutional provisions, treaties, international control, and even intervention in force, to uphold the rights of minorities, as seen in terms of numbers or of power, to have a say in their government, while preserving their own peculiar identity of language, religion, or culture.

This brief review will, it is hoped, have shown that the Declarations and Conventions after 1945[15] are not a wholly new departure, but are logical steps in old and continuing efforts for the protection and enforcement of human rights in many fields around the world, and that in these efforts a number of ideas and forces are at work. First, there is a persistent interaction between two principles, neither absolute: the fullest possible development of the individual, and the securing of the social order; and four broad standards have emerged: the rule of law, non-discrimination, self-determination, and the equality of men and women. The last is often expressed as a form of non-discrimination, but it perhaps deserves to stand alone.

Secondly, there is a distinction between rights and claims. When we speak of rights, we imply that there is, or ought to be, some means of their enforcement now. But there are countless human needs and human demands which ought to be met, but which can be met only in the future, either for material reasons, or because they are in conflict with each other and can only be properly met in the resolution of the conflict. These needs and demands are really claims, and we only manufacture difficulties if we try prematurely to treat them as rights.

Thirdly, experience shows that too narrow a view of the implementation of rights must be avoided. It is tempting to think always in terms of judicial process and of penal sanctions.

But the implementation of human rights has been attempted, not without success, in a number of ways, domestic and international, direct and indirect: domestic legislation and constitutional provisions, enforced in the courts;[16] regular reporting of progress in particular fields, country by country; fact-finding inquiries followed by expert recommendations; proceedings by way of petition or complaint; international sanctions, and even intervention, are all represented.

The essential feature of the Declarations and Conventions which we have listed is that they are the first endeavour to bring together, in the form of general but simple propositions that can be 'understanded of the people', the common rights of mankind, and that in some cases they go further and offer means of enforcement. Let us try to estimate the effectiveness of these Declarations and Conventions.

III

The Universal Declaration of Human Rights in 1948 did not, and was not designed to, establish contractual obligations between States; it rather laid down principles and standards. But its political impact, and its continuing fertility as a source of Conventions and constitutions,[17] are not to be underestimated. It has become an extension of the U.N. Charter itself. The implementation of human rights must, if it is to be effective, reach the individual in the end, and this need led the United Nations, through its Human Rights Commission, to attempt the transposition of the Universal Declaration into enforceable Covenants.

But the Declaration is a world document, which touches many different relations of individuals in and to the community, and reflects differing views of them. In one view these relations are to be defined and governed by rules of law or by principles that could be, but are not, translated into law.[18] Here the focus of human rights is the elimination of arbitrary restraints on the individual: his natural freedoms may be limited only in the interest of public order in the wide sense, and by action of the community, to which he can be said, however indirectly, to have consented. The limitations must be necessary, comprehensible, and fair. In the inherent possession of these rights the individual, in the words of the late Judge Sir Hersch Lauterpacht, 'as the ultimate unit of all law rises sovereign over the limited province of the State'. But this classical framework of civil and political rights, while it provides society with some essential securities, can leave it morally immobile. The man who stole bread was sure of a fair trial and was free to speak out in public against the law that condemned him, but he was still hanged.

So in the massive social movements from the mid-nineteenth century onwards other views of human rights emerged; that for the whole man civil liberties are not enough, that the relations of the individual and the community, of employers and workers, of men and women, must be adjusted so that each can get a fair livelihood, and enjoy decent conditions of life, and at the same time have the means of spiritual growth; and that the self-determination of whole peoples must be translated into direct political action. All these were in the beginning claims, to be established by the combined efforts of individuals and groups within the community, or in extreme cases by the construction of a whole new social order. In such an order civil and political rights might be no longer seen as inherent possessions, but as subjects of State grant, to be extended or reduced as the distant purposes of the social order were thought to require.[19]

The U.N. General Assembly reaffirmed the proposition that 'the enjoyment of civil and political freedoms and of economic, social and cultural rights are interconnected and interdependent',[20] and there was support in the debates of 1951, on how best to implement the Universal Declaration of 1948, for the drafting of a single enforceable Covenant of human rights. But the General Assembly came finally down on the side of two Covenants, one for civil and political rights, and the other for economic, social, and cultural rights. The arguments which carried the day were summarized by the U.N. Secretary-General to the effect 'that civil and political rights were enforceable, or justiciable, or of an "absolute" character, while economic, social and cultural rights were not or might not be; that the former were immediately applicable, while the latter were to be progressively implemented, and that, generally speaking, the former were rights of the individual "against" the State, while the latter were rights which the State would have to take positive action to promote'. A shorthand distinction was made on the same lines between 'legal' and 'programme' rights, the first being mandatory rules, and the second standards of approximation, a distinction analogous to that made in some modern constitutions between rules of law and 'directive principles'.

Now this distinction has an attractive, pragmatic look, and is certainly maintainable between a number of the rights dealt with in the Draft Covenants; but when it comes to choosing ways of implementing human rights there are important areas where it becomes blurred or breaks down. Let us take some examples, first where the distinction works, and then where it is of less help.

No one shall be subjected to torture or to cruel, inhuman or degrading treatment or punishment. . . .

Subject to any general law of the State concerned which provides for such reasonable restrictions as may be necessary to protect national security, public safety, health or morals, or the rights or freedoms of others, consistent with other rights recognized in this Covenant, (*a*) everyone legally within the territory of a State shall within that territory have the right to liberty of movement and freedom to choose his residence; (*b*) everyone shall be free to leave any country, including his own.

The States Parties to the Covenant, realizing that health is a state of complete physical, mental and social well-being, and not merely the absence of disease or infirmity, recognize the right of everyone to the enjoyment of the highest attainable standard of health.[21]

If we take these three provisions in turn, we see that the first two fall plainly into the category of 'legal' rights and that the third falls equally plainly among 'programme' rights. The first two rights are directly enforceable by means of legislation, judicial control, or administrative action, while the third is not enforceable at all in any practical sense of the term: it is a statement of a large social objective, to be attained only by inevitably slow and uneven advance on many fronts at once.

But the distinction does not adequately comprehend the fact that claims are, as the expression 'programme' rights implies, needs and demands in movement, and there is a continuous transformation, as a society advances, of economic and social claims into civil or political rights; and not all countries or all claims are by any means at the same stages in this process. Consider:

'No one shall be denied the right to education . . .'[22]

and

'The States Parties to the Covenant recognize the right of everyone to social security'.[23]

Without going into the question of what degree of State responsibility is expressed in these provisions, we must accept that, while in the majority of countries both are still 'programme' rights, in some industrialized countries they have been transformed not only into legal rights but even into legal obligations,[24] so that the means of implementation that would be appropriate in some countries would be quite inadequate in others.

Effectiveness of implementation of human rights depends then not only on the method itself, but on the choice of the right method for the kind of right or claim involved. Before we make a brief survey of methods, some general observations are necessary.

First, the reduction of even legal rights to short propositions can pose difficulties of interpretation for whoever has to implement them, be it a court, a commission of inquiry, or an expert investigator. Brevity does not necessarily mean precision, and may be only over-generalization. So, to take a simple example, it might seem at first sight that the expression 'inhuman treatment', in Article 3 of the European Convention on Human Rights, has an obvious meaning. But it is not so clear. Some might say that it is ill-treatment beyond the limits of characteristic human behaviour, such as genocide, torture, mass executions, but that it does not extend to the pain or even brutality that people inflict on each other in many situations; others would take a broader view and say that it covered any severe pain or suffering which was inflicted either unnecessarily or for its own sake.[25] The reader might reflect here on compulsory sterilization, and on where, in terms of inhuman treatment, a line is to be drawn, if it can, between racist practices of the Nazis, and recommendations which a eugenicist might honestly make for 'breeding out' defective human strains.

Secondly, the Declarations and Conventions are in great part concerned with the responsibility of States for the implementation of human rights. The Canadian jurist, Bora Laskin, has well said that they are primarily addressed to parliaments. They say little, perhaps too little, of the *obligations* of individuals, and they do not call for or cover either voluntary or private efforts to implement the various rights declared, save in so far as the State may be under a duty to support them out of public resources, nor do they prohibit individual action against human rights, save in so far as the State has a duty to prevent it.[26] What exactly the duty of the State is in these respects is often of course a matter of political controversy; for example, how far should the State intervene in labour relations and labour disputes, or organize medical care for part or all of its citizens, or by legislation outlaw racist activities? All these issues involve one or more of the provisions of the U.N. Covenants.

Thirdly, it is plain that to be a member of any community entails some restriction of freedom. Just as the co-existence of States on the international plane excludes the absolute sovereignty of any one of them, so a democratic State cannot itself survive with the unlimited autonomy of any individuals within it. It is generally accepted that the rights and freedoms of the individual may be restricted, at any rate where the restrictions are necessary to maintain the rights and freedoms of others, in other words, to maximize their enjoyment, or where the community is itself in danger. In any attempt to demarcate these orders of permitted restrictions, it is not on the one hand enough to provide simply that restrictions must conform with the law. So a constitution may well embody the rule that no one shall be deprived of his liberty otherwise than according to law; but this will be no protection of liberty at all if the legislature enacts a law authorizing detention without trial for renewable periods of three months. On the other hand, in any international control or supervision of restrictions of rights over freedoms, a government must be allowed a margin of appreciation of national needs. The European Convention endeavours to meet these difficulties by introducing the general criteria that restrictions on rights and freedoms, to be permissible, shall not only be prescribed by law but shall serve one or more defined social purposes, and shall be 'necessary in a democratic society';[27] that is to say, restriction of rights or freedoms must not be merely the administratively easy or convenient way, but the only way, of attaining that social purpose, and it must be imposed by general consent, through the action of a free and representative legislature or by some other democratic process. Again, where a government is entitled under the Convention to impose restrictions on rights or freedoms, in time of 'war or other public emergency threatening the life of the nation',[28] it would hardly be sensible to authorize an international body to be able freely to intervene and annul them; on the other hand, states of emergency can cover a multitude of sins. The

European Commission has endeavoured to strike a balance in saying that 'the Government should be able to exercise a certain measure of discretion in assessing the extent [of restriction] strictly required by the exigencies of the situation', but that the Commission remained 'competent to pronounce on the existence of a public danger which, under Article 15, would grant to the Contracting Party concerned, a right to derogate from the obligations laid down in the Convention'.

Finally, there are senses in which the implementation of human rights is always political, a fact which their static division into two categories tends to obscure. In the first place, where there is a denial of rights, the trouble usually lies far less in the personal malice or incompetence of some servant or officer of State than in the applicable *system*. Whether the denial takes the form, for example, of ill-treatment in prison, or unfair trial, or discrimination in public employment or in education, or restrictions on trade unions, or the breaking up of public meetings, there is in one way or another a general failure or defect in the method of public administration.

Secondly, the necessary remedy or reform may often be a matter of public controversy and debate, or even require legislation. Paradoxically perhaps, in the light of the distinction, it is the social and economic rights and claims which are the most political in this sense.

The choice and effectiveness of methods of implementation must be determined then by a number of large and complicated factors.

Periodic reports, such as appear in the U.N. *Yearbooks of Human Rights*, may describe the condition of human rights in a country as a whole, or particular features and developments. While accurate and informative as far as they go, they can be marked by a certain generality and complacency. More effective are annual country reports on progress in a particular field of human rights or in the application of particular Conventions. The I.L.O. has made great use of these by referring them to independent experts, who study them and make recommendations based on common standards.

Investigation on the spot, even if it is confined to fact-finding, is a more potent instrument, but it must always depend on at least the consent, if not the active co-operation, of the government of the country where it takes place. A government may, under an appearance of co-operation with the investigators, withhold evidence or prevent witnesses being heard or use its publicity machine to discredit the report or its conclusions. Further, many kinds of investigation call for special expertise, not always easy to mobilize.

It is generally recognized that, while systems of reports or investigations can often be effective, the most sure form of international implementation is the power to investigate specific complaints by individuals or groups.

All governments approach the grant of a right of individual petition to an international body with very great hesitation indeed, and it is perhaps remarkable that the right has been established at all and without limitation of nationality,[29] so that applicants to the European Commission can, and frequently do,[30] bring complaints of breaches of the Convention even against their own governments.[31]

The arguments against acceptance of the right of individual petition have been that it will lead to a mass of frivolous, paranoid, or generally baseless applications; or that it will be used to exploit political grievances or further political objectives that should be matters only for national parliaments; or that it undermines the authority of national courts by establishing a kind of appeal against their decisions; or that it embarrasses ordinary administration by introducing an incalculable element of review by an international body, which cannot easily appreciate all the domestic issues involved.

These arguments are not to be lightly dismissed, and have doubtless influenced countries, participating in the European Convention, not to make their acceptance of the right of individual petition irreversible.[32]

But the experience of the Commission, since its establishment in 1954, and of the European Court of Human Rights since 1958, suggests that the fears expressed in these arguments have not so far materialized, and the European Convention can be fairly said to be proving itself effective, even though its operation is rightly unspectacular.

But to set up such a system of international supervision or control in a region of common traditions and standards is one thing, to achieve it globally is another.

To attempt some broad conclusions, we may say that fundamental to all effective methods of implementation of human rights is independent and objective fact-finding, and its ally, publicity; indeed, publicity is perhaps the most decisive element of all.

The distinction between civil and political rights on the one hand and economic, social, and cultural rights on the other is only a rough criterion for sorting out human rights, and when it comes to their progressive implementation it has disadvantages; for it is a fixation of human rights in terms of a particular phase in the development of social ideas.

Notes

ESSAY I: NATURAL RIGHTS IN HOBBES AND LOCKE

1 References to the texts of Hobbes's works are given as follows: *Lev.* is *Leviathan*, with pages of the Oakeshott edition (1946); *El.* is *Elements of Law Natural and Politic*, Tönnies edition (1889); *Rud.* is *Philosophical Rudiments concerning Government and Society*, Lamprecht edition (published under the title *De Cive, or The Citizen*, 1949).

2 *Lev.*, Ch. 14, p. 86.

3 *Lev.*, Ch. 14, pp. 84–5. Cf. *El.*, I, Ch. 14, §§6–10; *Rud.*, Ch. 1, §§7–10.

4 *El.*, I, Ch. 14, §10, and *Rud.*, Ch. 1, §10.

5 *El.*, I, Ch. 14, §10.   6 *El.*, I, Ch. 14, §6; *Rud.*, Ch. 1, §7.

7 *El.*, I, Ch. 14, §§6–7.   8 *Rud.*, Ch. 1, §8.

9 *Rud.*, Ch. 1, §14.   10 *El.*, I, Ch. 8, §4.

11 *Lev.*, Ch. 8, p. 46; Ch. 11, p. 64; Ch. 13, p. 81; *El.*, I, Ch. 14, §3; *Rud.*, Ch. 1, §4.

12 This point is developed more fully in my *Political Theory of Possessive Individualism* (Oxford: Clarendon Press, 1962), pp. 40 ff., where I argue further that Hobbes's model of society was essentially the bourgeois market society.

13 *Lev.*, Ch. 15, pp. 100–1. Cf. *El.*, I, Ch. 17, §1; *Rud.*, Ch. 3, §13.

14 References to Locke's *Two Treatises of Government* are given as follows: 1T is *First Treatise*, 2T is *Second Treatise*; the following number is the section of the treatise, and the line numbers (ll.) are to the numbered lines of the section in the Laslett edition (1960).

15 2T, 6, l. 7. Cf. 2T, 25, l. 1.   16 1T, 86, ll. 27–8, 14, 15.

17 1T, 97, ll. 2–3.   18 E.g., 2T, 25, ll. 2–4.

19 1T, 86.   20 1T, 88, ll. 14–18.

21 1T, 86.   22 1T, 88, ll. 18–22.

23 2T, 4, ll. 3–6.   24 2T, 17, l. 9.

25 First introduced as a 'power' (2T, 7, l. 9), then called a right (2T, 17, l. 15).

26 2T, 11, ll. 1–3.   27 2T, 18.

28 2T, 4, ll. 7–16.   29 2T, 23, ll. 1–4.

30 2T, 6, ll. 9–10.   31 2T, 6, ll. 6–7.

32 *Lev.*, Ch. 14, p. 86.   33 2T, 23, l. 10.

34 2T, 25, ll. 16–19; 2T, 50, ll. 11–13.   35 2T, 25, ll. 2–4.

36 2T, 27, ll. 2–4. Cf. 2T, 44, l. 3.

37 *Political Theory of Possessive Individualism*, pp. 203–20.

38 2T, 50, l. 24.   39 2T, 37.   40 2T, 14, ll. 11–19.

41 2T, 37, l. 2.   42 2T, 37, l. 1.   43 2T, 50, ll. 11–14.

44 2T, 50, ll. 7–8.   45 2T, 48, ll. 21–2.

46 *Political Theory of Possessive Individualism*, p. 235.

47 2T, 123, ll. 6–13.   48 2T, 135, 137, 149.

49 'It is impossible for anyone to grow rich except at the expense of someone else.' *Essays on the Law of Nature*, ed. von Leyden (1954), p. 211.

50 Hobbes, who is generally thought to be more extreme in this matter than Locke, was I think really less so. For Hobbes postulated that only some men were by nature infinitely desirous (see note 11 above), whereas Locke's implicit assumption was that all men were naturally so. Locke attributes this infinite desire explicitly only to the second stage of the state of nature, but I think he assumed it also in man's original nature (see *Political Theory of Possessive Individualism*, pp. 234–5).

51 The writers of the French eighteenth-century Enlightenment did assume that men could be changed, but only *to* the bourgeois model (which they thought men had not yet attained), not beyond it. And their theories consequently depended less on natural rights than on a concept of a natural order, or utility.

52 This is demonstrated in *Political Theory of Possessive Individualism*, Ch. II, Section 3, §§i–iv.

ESSAY II: THE RIGHTS OF MAN IN HOBBES AND LOCKE

1 Rousseau, *Social Contract*, Bk. I, Ch. 4.

2 Hobbes, *Leviathan* (ed. Molesworth, *English Works*, Vol. III, 1839), Ch. 13, p. 115.

3 Hobbes, *Elements of Law*, Pt. I, Ch. 4, §11. *De Homine*, Ch. 10, §5.

4 *Leviathan*, Ch. 14, p. 117.   5 *Ibid.*, p. 118.

6 *Ibid.*, Ch. 15, p. 131.

7 Spinoza, *Tractatus Theologico-Politicus* (ed. Gebhardt, Vol. III, 1925), Ch. 16, pp. 189–90.

8 Hobbes, *Leviathan*, Ch. 13, p. 115.

⁹ *Ibid.*, Ch. 14, pp. 118–19, and Ch. 15, p. 141.

¹⁰ *Ibid.*, Ch. 17, p. 158.   ¹¹ *Ibid.*, Ch. 14, p. 116.

¹² *Ibid.*, Ch. 14, p. 117.   ¹³ *Ibid.*, Ch. 13, p. 115.

¹⁴ Cf. my article, 'Justice et Raison chez Hobbes', *Rivista critica dell' istoria della filosofia*, 1963, pp. 450 ff.

¹⁵ Hobbes, *De Cive*, Ch. 1, §7, and *Leviathan*, Ch. 15, p. 147.

¹⁶ Hobbes, *Leviathan*, Ch. 14, p. 117.

¹⁷ Hobbes, *De Cive*, Ch. 1, §1, note of 1646, and *Leviathan*, Ch. 15, p. 147.

¹⁸ Hobbes, *Leviathan*, Ch. 15, p. 141.

¹⁹ *Ibid.*, Ch. 21, p. 208, Ch. 27, p. 279, and Ch. 28, p. 297.

²⁰ *Ibid.*, Ch. 14, p. 120.   ²¹ *Ibid.*, Ch. 14, p. 127.

²² *Ibid.*, Ch. 14, p. 120. One can recognize in the passage the principle of the Fifth Amendment of the American Constitution.

²³ Robert Filmer, *Observations on Mr. Hobbes's Leviathan (Patriarcha and Other Political Works*, ed. Laslett, 1949), Ch. 15, p. 248.

²⁴ *Ibid.*, pp. 241–2.

²⁵ Locke, *Second Treatise of Civil Government*, §57.

²⁶ *Ibid.*, §61.   ²⁷ *Ibid.*, §§59 and 60.

²⁸ *Ibid.*, §§6, 7, and 87.   ²⁹ *Ibid.*, §§4 and 57.

³⁰ *Ibid.*, §58.   ³¹ *Ibid.*, §17.   ³² *Ibid.*, §8.

³³ *Ibid.*, §10.   ³⁴ *Ibid.*, §63.

³⁵ *Ibid.*, §§8, 10, 11, and 129.

³⁶ Locke, *Epistola de Tolerantia* (ed. Klibansky and Polin, 1961), p. 72.

³⁷ Locke, *First Treatise*, §39.

³⁸ Locke, *Essay concerning Human Understanding*, Bk. IV, Ch. 3, §18.

³⁹ Locke, *Second Treatise*, §87.   ⁴⁰ *Ibid.*, §123.

⁴¹ *Ibid.*, §§87 and 123.   ⁴² *Ibid.*, §45.   ⁴³ *Ibid.*, §31.

⁴⁴ *Ibid.*, §194.   ⁴⁵ *Ibid.*, §26.   ⁴⁶ *Ibid.*, §§27 and 28.

⁴⁷ *Ibid.*, §36.   ⁴⁸ *Ibid.*, §§23 and 135.   ⁴⁹ *Ibid.*, §23.

⁵⁰ *Ibid.*, §195.   ⁵¹ *Ibid.*, §91.   ⁵² *Ibid.*, §23.

ESSAY III: NATURAL RIGHTS AND JUSTICE IN LIBERALISM

¹ 'Post-Liberal-Democracy?', *Canadian Journal of Economics and Political Science*, XXX (Nov. 1964), 485–98, p. 498.

² *The Political Theory of Possessive Individualism* (Oxford: Clarendon Press, 1962), p. 271.

3 'Natural Rights in Hobbes and Locke', Essay I in this volume, p. 4.
4 *Ibid.*, p. 10.   5 *Ibid.*, p. 11.
6 *Political Theory of Possessive Individualism*, pp. 55-6.
7 *Ibid.*, p. 56.
8 'Natural Rights in Hobbes and Locke', pp. 4-5. 'Each writer's theory of natural rights was determined by his postulate about the nature of man.' *Ibid.*, p. 12.
9 *Political Theory of Possessive Individualism*, p. 221.
10 'Natural Rights in Hobbes and Locke', p. 9.   11 *Ibid.*, p. 12.
12 John Rawls, 'Justice as Fairness', *The Philosophical Review*, LXVII (April 1958), 164-94, p. 165.
13 See Abram Bergson, *Essays in Normative Economics* (Cambridge, Mass.: Belknap Press, 1966), especially the essay 'On Social Welfare Once More', pp. 51-77, in which Bergson presents a criterion of social welfare that incorporates a more 'contractarian' concept of justice than the utilitarian one on which Macpherson appears to rely.
14 Bernard Williams, 'The Idea of Equality', in Peter Laslett and W. G. Runciman (Eds.), *Philosophy, Politics and Society (Second Series)*, (Oxford: Basil Blackwell, 1962), 110-31, p. 121.
15 'Natural Rights in Hobbes and Locke', p. 15.
16 Lee Soltow, *Toward Income Equality in Norway* (Madison: University of Wisconsin Press, 1965), p. 110.
17 'The Deceptive Task of Political Theory', *Cambridge Journal*, VII (June 1954), 560-8, p. 567. He refers also to 'a revolution in democratic consciousness' in 'Post-Liberal-Democracy?', p. 498, and to 'some kind of moral or social transformation' in 'Natural Rights in Hobbes and Locke', p. 12.
18 See my 'Political Theory: Logical Structure and Enduring Types', in Raymond Polin (Ed.), *L'Idée de philosophie politique* (Paris: Presses Universitaires de France, 1965), pp. 57-96, and 'Formative and Emergent Types of Political Theory', *Rajavidya*, 3 (Dec. 1964), pp. 1-14.
19 *Problems of Historical Psychology* (London: Routledge & Kegan Paul, 1960), p. 209.
20 ' "Chosisme": A Socio-psychological Interpretation', *European Journal of Sociology*, IV (1963), 127-47, p. 143.
21 John Plamenatz, *Man and Society* (London: Longmans; New York: McGraw-Hill, 1963), Vol. II, p. 456.
22 'Conservative and Prosthetic Justice', *Political Studies*, XII (June, 1964), 149-62, pp. 161-2.

23 'The Politics of Consensus in an Age of Affluence', *The American Political Science Review*, LIX (Dec. 1965), 874–95, p. 877.

24 *The Future of Political Science* (New York: Atherton Press, 1963), p. 118.

25 For moral freedom in the shape of 'individual ideals', see P. F. Strawson, 'Social Morality and Individual Ideal', *Philosophy*, XXXVI (Jan. 1961), pp. 1–17.

26 *The Political Theory of Possessive Individualism*, p. 270.

27 *Ibid.*, p. 251.

28 Kenneth E. Boulding, 'Social Justice in Social Dynamics', in Richard B. Brandt (Ed.), *Social Justice* (Englewood Cliffs, N.J.: Prentice-Hall, 1962), 73–92, p. 90.

29 William K. Frankena, 'The Concept of Social Justice', in R. B. Brandt (Ed.), *Social Justice*, 1–29, p. 16.

ESSAY IV: HUMAN RIGHTS, REAL AND SUPPOSED

1 Arthur L. Corbin in his Introduction to Hohfield's *Fundamental Legal Conceptions* (Yale U.P., New Haven, 1964).

2 *Anarchical Fallacies.*

3 *The Philosophy of Edmund Burke*, ed. Bredvold and Ross (Michigan U.P., Ann Arbor, 1960), p. 205.

4 C. J. Friedrich, in 'Rights, Liberties, Freedoms: A Reappraisal', *American Political Science Review*, LVII, 4, (Dec. 1963), shows that some 'social and economic rights' were known to the Age of Reason. He quotes the 'right to work' being named by Turgot and Robespierre, and gives references to eighteenth-century claims to the right to education.

5 E.g., Professor C. J. Friedrich (cf. previous note). Another champion of the view that social and economic rights should be interpreted as human rights is the late Pope, John XXIII. I have discussed his views in an article, 'Pope John XXIII on Peace and the Rights of Man', *Political Quarterly*, Oct. 1963.

6 See A. H. Robertson, *Human Rights in Europe* (Manchester U.P., 1964).

7 See G. Sartori, 'Constitutionalism', *American Political Science Review*, Vol. LVI (Dec. 1962), pp. 853–65.

ESSAY VI: WHAT ARE HUMAN RIGHTS?

1 Apart from the preceding essay by Professor Raphael, I refer in particular to: Margaret Macdonald, 'Natural Rights', *Proceedings of the Aristotelian Society*, 1946–7; H. L. A. Hart, 'Are there any Natural Rights?' and Stuart M. Brown, 'Inalienable Rights' (independent papers), discussed by William K. Frankena, 'Natural and Inalienable Rights', in *Philosophical Review*, LXIV (1955), pp. 175–232.

2 H. L. A. Hart, *The Concept of Law* (1961), IX, 2.

3 *Loc. cit.*, p. 197.   4 *Loc. cit.*, pp. 175, 193.

5 Also Hart (*loc. cit.*, p. 179), who calls it a 'minimum' and not 'centrally important' sense of 'right'.

6 *Loc. cit.*, p. 185.   7 Cf. M. Macdonald, *op. cit.*, p. 47.

ESSAY IX: THE RIGHTS OF MAN AND THE RIGHTS OF THE CITIZEN

1 Cf. *Lectures* (on Justice, etc.) *of Adam Smith*, ed. E. Cannan (1896), pp. 5–6. There is a fuller account in an as yet unpublished manuscript.

2 See *A Documentary History of Socialist Thought*, ed. A. Fried and R. Sanders (1964), p. 66.

3 Part II, Ch. 5; Everyman edition (1915), pp. 250–1.

4 *The Writings of Thomas Paine*, ed. M. D. Conway (1895), Vol. III, p. 331.

5 *Ibid.*, pp. 337–9.

6 *Observations on the More Ancient Statutes* (1769), p. 480. I am indebted to Mr. F. W. Jessup, Fellow of Wolfson College, Oxford, for drawing my attention to this passage.

7 *Ibid.*, p. 481.

ESSAY X: THE INTERNATIONAL PROTECTION OF HUMAN RIGHTS

1 There appears to be no clear distinction in general usage between 'human', 'natural', and 'fundamental' rights. 'Common rights' as an alternative has an appealing echo of the common law.

2 See A. P. d'Entrèves, *Natural Law* (1951).

3 *Somersett's Case* [1772].   4 *Le Louis* [1817] 2 Dods. 210.

5 The treaties of protection, which Great Britain concluded from 1820 onwards in the Persian Gulf, also stemmed in large part from

efforts to suppress the slave trade. For later measures on slavery, see the
Slavery Convention, 1926, and *Supplementary Convention on the
Abolition of Slavery*, 1956.

⁶ Article 23*a*.

⁷ Among Conventions those more particularly concerned with
'human rights' in the sense of the U.N. Declaration of 1948 are:
Minimum Wage (Industry), 1919, and *(Sea)*, 1920; *Right of Association (Agriculture)*, 1921; *Freedom of Association*, 1948 (70); *Right to
Organize and Collective Bargaining*, 1949 (81); *Equal Remuneration*,
1951 (51); *Discrimination (Employment and Occupation) Convention*,
1958, (51). The figures in brackets are the numbers of States parties.

⁸ See, for example, the observation of the U.S. Supreme Court on
the I.L.O. *Shipowners' Liability Convention*, 1936: 'The aim indeed
was not to change materially American standards but to equalize
operating costs by raising the standards of member nations to the
American level': *Warren* v. *United States* [1951] 340 U.S. 523.

⁹ Not confined to European States: see C. H. Alexandrowicz, 'A
Persian-Dutch Treaty in the XVIIth Century', *Indian Yearbook of
International Affairs*, 1958, p. 1.

¹⁰ See principle formulated by Asian-African Legal Consultative
Committee at Colombo, 1960: *Third Session Report*, p. 155. For
practice in Eastern Europe, see A. Drucker, 'Communist Compensation Treaties', 10 *International and Comparative Law Quarterly* (April
1961), 238. See generally also U.N. General Assembly Resolution
1803–XVII (Permanent Sovereignty over Natural Resources).

¹¹ *Status of Refugees Convention*, 1951. See also *European Extradition Convention*, 1960, Article 3.

¹² Only A mandates obtained early independence.

¹³ See U.N. Charter, Articles 73*b*, 76*b*.

¹⁴ Resolution 1514–XIV, adopted by 90–0 with 9 abstentions.

¹⁵ These may be grouped as follows: (ratifications in parenthises)
United Nations: *Genocide Convention*, 1948 (67).

> *Universal Declaration of Human Rights*, 1948; and *Draft
> Covenants on Civil and Political Rights, and Economic, Social
> and Cultural Rights.*
> *Status of Refugees Convention*, 1951 (48).
> *Convention on Political Rights of Women*, 1952 (45).
> *Declaration on Granting of Independence*, 1960.
> *Declaration on the Prevention of Racial Discrimination*, 1965;
> and Draft Convention.

UNESCO: *Convention on Discrimination in Education*, 1960 (31).
European Convention on Human Rights, 1950 (16).
Inter-American Convention on Human Rights, 1960.

The four Geneva *Conventions for the Protection of War Victims*, 1949, are also important codifications of rules of conduct in armed conflict; for their application by the United Kingdom, see *Geneva Conventions Act*, 1957.

[16] The *European Convention on Human Rights* has in West Germany, Austria, Belgium, and the Netherlands the status of domestic law, and can be invoked in the courts.

[17] E.g., the *European Convention on Human Rights*, and provisions in the constitutions of India, Nigeria, and Sierra Leone.

[18] The British preference for agreed working principles over formal legislation, though both have the same function, is illustrated by constitutional 'conventions', and by the Judges' Rules on criminal investigation.

[19] See B. M. Peselj, 'Recent Codification of Human Rights in Socialist Constitutions', 11 *Howard Law Journal* (Spring 1965), 345.

[20] Resolution 421–V.

[21] The first two are *Draft Covenant on Civil and Political Rights*, Articles 7 and 12(1); the third is *Draft Covenant on Economic, Social and Cultural Rights*, Article 13 (1): little changed in final Covenants, 1966.

[22] *European Convention on Human Rights*, Protocol, Article 2.

[23] *Draft Covenant on Economic, Social and Cultural Rights*, Article 9.

[24] This last has led to a curious problem of conflict of rights before the European Commission of Human Rights, when certain members of the Dutch Reformed Church applied to it, claiming that compulsory old-age insurance in the Netherlands interfered with their freedom to perform their religious duty, as protected by Article 9 of the European Convention, that is, to care for their aged folk themselves as commanded in the Bible: for the rejection of the claim by the Commission, see *Yearbook of the European Convention*, V (1962), 296.

[25] These and intermediate views have been considered in the European Commission of Human Rights on particular facts revealed in petitions made to it.

[26] For the principle that there can be no right or freedom to undermine or take away the rights and freedoms of others, see *European Convention*, Article 17.

[27] See second paragraphs of Articles 8–11.

28 Article 51(1). But even in these situations certain derogations from the Convention are forbidden: Article 15(2).

29 *European Convention on Human Rights*, Article 25, accepted by Austria, Belgium, Denmark, Federal Republic of Germany, Iceland, Ireland, Luxembourg, Netherlands, Norway, Sweden, United Kingdom. Greece, Italy, Turkey, and Cyprus have not yet accepted it.

30 Nearly 3,000 individual applications have been received since 1954, not, however, a large number from eleven countries in twelve years.

31 This is not wholly without parallel. The I.L.O Committee on Freedom of Association, established in 1951, has since then dealt with about three hundred complaints of violation of trade union rights, in addition to carrying out on-the-spot inquiries at the request of governments concerned, for example in Malaya and Burma in 1962, and Japan in 1965.

32 Most countries accept for periods of three or five years at a time, acceptance being renewable. Iceland, Ireland, and Sweden have accepted without time-limit. The acceptance by the United Kingdom runs until 14 January 1969, when it will be renewable. No country is obliged under the Convention to renew its acceptance, though none has yet failed to do so.

Appendix

UNIVERSAL DECLARATION OF HUMAN RIGHTS

Adopted and proclaimed by the General Assembly of the United Nations on 10 *December* 1948

PREAMBLE

Whereas recognition of the inherent dignity and of the equal and inalienable rights of all members of the human family is the foundation of freedom, justice and peace in the world,

Whereas disregard and contempt for human rights have resulted in barbarous acts which have outraged the conscience of mankind, and the advent of a world in which human beings shall enjoy freedom of speech and belief and freedom from fear and want has been proclaimed as the highest aspiration of the common people,

Whereas it is essential, if man is not to be compelled to have recourse, as a last resort, to rebellion against tyranny and oppression, that human rights should be protected by the rule of law,

Whereas it is essential to promote the development of friendly relations between nations,

Whereas the peoples of the United Nations have in the Charter reaffirmed their faith in fundamental human rights, in the dignity and worth of the human person and in the equal rights of men and women and have determined to promote social progress and better standards of life in larger freedom,

Whereas Member States have pledged themselves to achieve, in co-operation with the United Nations, the promotion of universal respect for and observance of human rights and fundamental freedoms,

Whereas a common understanding of these rights and freedoms is of the greatest importance for the full realization of this pledge,

Now, Therefore,

THE GENERAL ASSEMBLY

proclaims

THIS UNIVERSAL DECLARATION OF HUMAN RIGHTS as a common standard of achievement for all peoples and all nations, to the end that every individual and every organ of society, keeping this Declaration constantly in mind, shall strive by teaching and education to promote respect for these rights and freedoms and by progressive measures, national and international, to secure their universal and effective recognition and observance, both among the peoples of Member States themselves and among the peoples of territories under their jurisdiction.

Article 1. All human beings are born free and equal in dignity and rights. They are endowed with reason and conscience and should act towards one another in a spirit of brotherhood.

Article 2. Everyone is entitled to all the rights and freedoms set forth in this Declaration, without distinction of any kind, such as race, colour, sex, language, religion, political or other opinion, national or social origin, property, birth or other status.

Furthermore, no distinction shall be made on the basis of the political, jurisdictional or international status of the country or territory to which a person belongs, whether it be independent, trust, non-self-governing or under any other limitation of sovereignty.

Article 3. Everyone has the right to life, liberty and security of person.

Article 4. No one shall be held in slavery or servitude; slavery and the slave trade shall be prohibited in all their forms.

Article 5. No one shall be subjected to torture or to cruel, inhuman or degrading treatment or punishment.

Article 6. Everyone has the right to recognition everywhere as a person before the law.

Article 7. All are equal before the law and are entitled without any discrimination to equal protection of the law. All are entitled to equal protection against any discrimination in violation of this Declaration and against any incitement to such discrimination.

Article 8. Everyone has the right to an effective remedy by the competent national tribunals for acts violating the fundamental rights granted him by the constitution or by law.

Article 9. No one shall be subjected to arbitrary arrest, detention or exile.

Article 10. Everyone is entitled in full equality to a fair and public hearing by an independent and impartial tribunal, in the determination of his rights and obligations and of any criminal charge against him.

Article 11. (1) Everyone charged with a penal offence has the right to be presumed innocent until proved guilty according to law in a public trial at which he has had all the guarantees necessary for his defence.

(2) No one shall be held guilty of any penal offence on account of any act or omission which did not constitute a penal offence, under national or international law, at the time when it was committed. Nor shall a heavier penalty be imposed than the one that was applicable at the time the penal offence was committed.

Article 12. No one shall be subjected to arbitrary interference with his privacy, family, home or correspondence, nor to attacks upon his honour and reputation. Everyone has the right to the protection of the law against such interference or attacks.

Article 13. (1) Everyone has the right to freedom of movement and residence within the borders of each state.

(2) Everyone has the right to leave any country, including his own, and to return to his country.

Article 14. (1) Everyone has the right to seek and to enjoy in other countries asylum from persecution.

(2) This right may not be invoked in the case of prosecutions genuinely arising from non-political crimes or from acts contrary to the purposes and principles of the United Nations.

Article 15. (1) Everyone has the right to a nationality.

(2) No one shall be arbitrarily deprived of his nationality nor denied the right to change his nationality.

Article 16. (1) Men and women of full age, without any limitation due to race, nationality or religion, have the right to marry and to found a family. They are entitled to equal rights as to marriage, during marriage and at its dissolution.

(2) Marriage shall be entered into only with the free and full consent of the intending spouses.

(3) The family is the natural and fundamental group unit of society and is entitled to protection by society and the State.

Article 17. (1) Everyone has the right to own property alone as well as in association with others.

(2) No one shall be arbitrarily deprived of his property.

Article 18. Everyone has the right to freedom of thought, conscience and religion; this right includes freedom to change his religion or belief, and freedom, either alone or in community with others and in public or private, to manifest his religion or belief in teaching, practice, worship and observance.

Article 19. Everyone has the right to freedom of opinion and expression; this right includes freedom to hold opinions without interference and to seek, receive and impart information and ideas through any media and regardless of frontiers.

Article 20. (1) Everyone has the right to freedom of peaceful assembly and association.

(2) No one may be compelled to belong to an association.

Article 21. (1) Everyone has the right to take part in the government of his country, directly or through freely chosen representatives.

(2) Everyone has the right of equal access to public service in his country.

(3) The will of the people shall be the basis of the authority of government; this will shall be expressed in periodic and genuine elections which shall be by universal and equal suffrage and shall be held by secret vote or by equivalent free voting procedures.

Article 22. Everyone, as a member of society, has the right to social security and is entitled to realization, through national effort and international co-operation and in accordance with the organization and resources of each State, of the economic, social and cultural rights indispensable for his dignity and the free development of his personality.

Article 23. (1) Everyone has the right to work, to free choice of employment, to just and favourable conditions of work and to protection against unemployment.

(2) Everyone, without any discrimination, has the right to equal pay for equal work.

(3) Everyone who works has the right to just and favourable remuneration ensuring for himself and his family an existence worthy of human dignity, and supplemented, if necessary, by other means of social protection.

(4) Everyone has the right to form and to join trade unions for the protection of his interests.

Article 24. Everyone has the right to rest and leisure, including reasonable limitation of working hours and periodic holidays with pay.

Article 25. (1) Everyone has the right to a standard of living adequate for the health and well-being of himself and of his family, including food, clothing, housing and medical care and necessary social services, and the right to security in the event of unemployment, sickness, disability, widowhood, old age or other lack of livelihood in circumstances beyond his control.

(2) Motherhood and childhood are entitled to special care and assistance. All children, whether born in or out of wedlock, shall enjoy the same social protection.

Article 26. (1) Everyone has the right to education. Education shall be free, at least in the elementary and fundamental stages. Elementary education shall be compulsory. Technical and professional education shall be made generally available and higher education shall be equally accessible to all on the basis of merit.

(2) Education shall be directed to the full development of the human personality and to the strengthening of respect for human rights and fundamental freedoms. It shall promote understanding, tolerance and friendship among all nations, racial or religious groups, and shall further the activities of the United Nations for the maintenance of peace.

(3) Parents have a prior right to choose the kind of education that shall be given to their children.

Article 27. (1) Everyone has the right freely to participate in the cultural life of the community, to enjoy the arts and to share in scientific advancement and its benefits.

(2) Everyone has the right to the protection of the moral and material interests resulting from any scientific, literary or artistic production of which he is the author.

Article 28. Everyone is entitled to a social and international order in which the rights and freedoms set forth in this Declaration can be fully realized.

Article 29. (1) Everyone has duties to the community in which alone the free and full development of his personality is possible.

(2) In the exercise of his rights and freedoms, everyone shall be subject only to such limitations as are determined by law solely for the purpose of securing due recognition and respect for the rights and freedoms of others and of meeting the just requirements of morality, public order and the general welfare in a democratic society.

(3) These rights and freedoms may in no case be exercised contrary to the purposes and principles of the United Nations.

Article 30. Nothing in this Declaration may be interpreted as implying for any State, group or person any right to engage in any activity or to perform any act aimed at the destruction of any of the rights and freedoms set forth herein.

Index